DON'T PANIC!

DON'T PANIC!

ALL THE STUFF THE EXPECTANT DAD NEEDS TO KNOW

GEORGE LEWIS

monoray

Medical disclaimer

While all reasonable care has been taken in the preparation of this book the information it contains is not intended to take the place of advice from or treatment by a qualified medical practitioner. If you have concerns about your own or your baby's health, you must seek professional advice. Any reliance on the information contained in this book is at the reader's sole discretion and risk.

First published in Great Britain in 2022 by Monoray, an imprint of
Octopus Publishing Group Ltd
Carmelite House
50 Victoria Embankment
London EC4Y 0DZ
www.octopusbooks.co.uk
www.octopusbooksusa.com

An Hachette UK Company
www.hachette.co.uk

Distributed in the US by Hachette Book Group
1290 Avenue of the Americas , 4th and 5th Floors
New York, NY 10104

Distributed in Canada by Canadian Manda Group
664 Annette St., Toronto, Ontario, Canada M6S 2C8

ISBN 978-1-80096-008-4

A CIP catalogue record for this book is available from the British Library.

Printed and bound in the United Kingdom

10 9 8 7 6 5 4 3 2 1

This FSC® label means that materials used for the product have been responsibly sourced

MIX
Paper from
responsible sources
FSC
www.fsc.org   FSC® C104740

CONTENTS

INTRODUCTION

YOU'RE GOING TO BE A DAD. DON'T PANIC!

Before you have kids, it feels like every parent you know constantly says to you, 'It's the best thing you'll ever do.' Then, when you tell them you are going to have one, they give you a smile that says, 'Unlucky, sucker!' That's when the panic sets in.

It can feel like your whole life is about to change and you need to learn everything there is to know about how to be a dad in a very short amount of time.

But it's going to be absolutely fine, mate. The thing that helped me most when I was going through it for the first time was to have friends who could fill me in on what's what; other dads who were a few steps ahead of me on the same path who could say, 'Don't worry too much about that bit' or 'Oh yeah, that's horrible, isn't it?' or 'Get that checked *right now*! Look at the colour of it!'

This book is not a definitive guide to the best way of doing things. It's not a medical book by any stretch of the imagination and it's not always backed up by science (or even logic). But it will give you a very good idea of all of the stuff you need to do, and some of the things my friends and I learned might help you not to mess up your kid so much that they run off and join a cult.

I'm a normal person who works as a comedian and I spend my days writing jokes for TV shows and silly articles about football, and my evenings driving around the country to try to make strangers laugh. But none of those things prepares you for fatherhood. Apart from a helpful anonymous midwife and Adam Kay, who is an actual doctor, all of my friends who have contributed to this book are successful comedians, but when it comes to being parents, they are all going through the same things you will go through. They all felt underqualified for it, just like I did and just like you will. We had to learn most things on the job and had lots of moments where we got it wrong or thought we wouldn't be able to do it. But we did. And you can too.

Hopefully that hasn't got you so pumped up with confidence that you've slammed the book shut and strutted away into fatherhood, because there are quite a few things you need to know first.

ALL OF THE DADS

My situation is what some people might consider 'traditional' and some others might consider 'the most painfully dull and unimaginative thing in the world': I have a wife and two kids. But, as anyone who has ever stayed the night with another family knows, no family is normal.

Dads come in all shapes and sizes. There are young dads, old dads, stepdads, foster dads, rich dads, poor dads, dads who never thought they wanted to be dads and dads who never thought they could. Some dads are straight, some dads are gay, some dads aren't called Dad. There are separated dads and dads who are going to separate. There are stay-at-home dads, work-away dads, co-parenting dads, single dads and dads who can't see their kids. You might be a completely different dad altogether. Whatever dad you are – or are going to be – you will have a lot in common with the rest of us. And when we share our experiences of fatherhood, we can really help one another.

There may even be some mums who read this. And to you I say, welcome. Have a look around, enjoy yourself. We've got nothing to hide. But you probably don't want to waste your time with the 'Dad Tricks' sections. There really is nothing of interest in there so, if I were you, I'd just skip right past those. OK? Good.

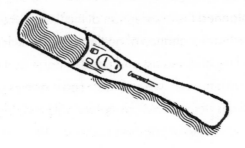

CHAPTER 1

PREGNANCY

Every future dad reacts differently when he hears the words, 'I'm pregnant'. You might punch the air, burst into tears, feel like you want to shout it from the rooftops or pretend it's not happening. You might feel relief, you might feel dread, you might feel nothing. No emotion is right or wrong and you will probably go through loads of them in the next few weeks, so don't attach too much to the first one you feel.

RUSSELL KANE: I was weirdly serene when I found out I was going to become a dad. I'd planned the conception to the day and, when Lindsey walked in with the blue line on a stick, I just thought: indeed, we're on schedule. We even planned the conception at the time of the month to give the highest chance of getting a girl. We desperately wanted a girl. As sexist and gender-norm as it sounds in these modern times, we both hate sport, armies and all the lame things boys like. My daughter will probably grow up to play for England knowing my luck.

IAIN STIRLING: I ran laps around the dining room table, absolutely delighted. A few hours later I played some FIFA on my PlayStation, realized I wouldn't be able to do this in a year's time and had a mild panic attack. In all honesty, I felt ready. It's a really exciting feeling to be fair. The first time I've ever had a job coming up that I truly felt ready for. Properly prepared, like I'm built for it. But when I told other fathers this, they all looked at me the same way. The way you look at a five-year-old who's just told you they still believe in Santa. A look that suggested my naivety was astonishing and in a mere couple of weeks I would be tired, crying and covered in another human's shit. I just hoped they were wrong. I hoped all 57 of them were wrong.

ARE YOU SURE SHE'S PREGNANT?

To be holding this book I suspect your answer is: pretty sure mate, yes.

But during the first part of the pregnancy, it will be something you doubt at several points. You might have expected that after you'd seen the blue line on the test, you'd then go to a doctor to get it confirmed, but no. After you've had your positive test, there is no interaction with a medical professional until eight weeks later, other than a quick appointment with the GP to get you 'into the system'. Even then, all a midwife will do with your partner is go through her medical history, check her height, weight and blood pressure, do a blood test and take a urine sample. They usually don't do a test to prove whether or not she is actually pregnant until the 12-week scan. That's three months just relying on your own medical conclusion! And how many PhDs do you have? So, prepare yourself for a strange period where you constantly question everything.

Your partner will probably have a better idea about the whole thing because she'll start having pregnancy-related symptoms, such as nausea, fatigue and a weird taste in her mouth, so she might get annoyed by you questioning it. But even she will have her doubts at times. If it gets too much, in the UK, you have the option of paying for an early scan. Or you can do what we did and refuse to go for one of these but spend the equivalent money on extra pregnancy tests every time you do a big shop.

DAD TRICK Buy the expensive pregnancy test for the initial one, then a shitload of cheap ones to have in the house. You can get them for a couple of quid in the supermarket. I can't tell you how many times you'll want to do another to double-check if she is actually pregnant and these will give you the reassurance you need. If you go with Clearblue for every test, you'll have no money for nappies when the baby arrives.

The uncertainty got so much for us that we managed to convince a midwife in the family to borrow a Doppler (a tool for listening to baby's heartbeat) from work and have a listen the next time we saw her, which happened to be Christmas Day. She was initially reluctant, which at the time we couldn't understand. What could be more perfect than hearing new life on Christmas morning? It'd be like our own little nativity scene. But I realized why she had her reservations when, a couple of minutes into her investigation, she couldn't find the heartbeat.

She was trying to wear an expression that everything was absolutely fine, but broke character when Uncle Terry came into the room with a bottle of Buck's Fizz and said, 'Merry Christm—' and she snapped, 'Terry, just fuck off for a minute!' This definitely wasn't like the nativity.

Luckily, it was as if the baby sensed the tension and immediately wriggled into a position to reveal its heartbeat. Everything was instantly OK and Terry was told to crack open his bottle.

The baby was still the size of a strawberry at this point, so it's easy to see why it might be tricky to find the heartbeat, but it's very hard to use the logic of fruit when you're sitting there in complete silence fearing the worst. This was one of many more worries to come. But thankfully, the worries you experience far outweigh the likelihood that anything will go wrong.

ASSISTED CONCEPTION

The process of getting pregnant is not a level playing field. For some people it can take seconds and for some it can take years. Some use *in vitro* fertilization (IVF) or surrogacy, either because they have found it difficult to get pregnant or, like Jen Brister, because they are part of a same-sex couple.

JEN BRISTER: If I can give any couple advice when it comes to IVF it's this: looking for any reassurance from a fertility clinic is like expecting a coherent answer from Mystic Meg.

It quickly became clear to both of us that IVF is not an exact science. In fact, it would be fair to say that they don't really know what the hell they're doing. The whole process is so frustrating and demoralizing I'm surprised we don't see more ovulating women dancing naked under a full moon shaking some lucky heather in the air out of sheer desperation.

I still find it astounding that when so much money and heartache is at stake, we put all our faith in a science which is about as precise as watching two toddlers play Velcro darts while blindfolded.

Being the 'other' parent is a weird position to be in, because it doesn't really matter how committed you are to 'the process' or to your partner, when you're not the one trying to get pregnant it's hard to stay 100 per cent connected; there is a disconnect with what is happening to your partner (everything) and what is happening to you (absolutely nothing). Naturally, a little part of your brain will start to shut down, or at least a bit of mine did.

I tried to be 'present' and supportive during my girlfriend's IVF treatment, and I think for the most part I was. I just wasn't really necessary to the entire proceedings. Or any of the proceedings. What I'm saying is, at this point I felt surplus to requirements.

It's a weird place to find yourself in because, as I became more invested in the idea of becoming a parent, I became more aware of how nothing I did, or didn't do, could affect the final outcome.

Trying for a baby is all-consuming, even if you consider yourself to be the most pragmatic, dispassionate and objective person on the planet. Once you start the process, the stakes accelerate to stratospherically high very quickly.

That imaginary baby that you felt no real attachment to at the beginning suddenly becomes your everything. It didn't seem to matter that we had been perfectly happy without a baby, that we enjoyed our jobs, our friends, our social life, our independence. Now all we wanted was a baby, with no real understanding of what having a baby meant.

My advice is, if you can talk to anyone who has already been through the process, then do it. There is so much obfuscation that it can be frustrating and disheartening when it doesn't work the first, second or even third time around. And if you feel like the clinic you're with isn't working for you, don't stay with them; our first clinic was a disaster and I'm positive we would never have conceived had we stayed with them. Follow your instincts and, lastly, DON'T TELL ANYONE you're going through it, unless you want people asking you every time you meet up whether you're pregnant yet. Eventually you will want to punch them in the face, even if you are pregnant.

SHARING YOUR NEWS

Obviously, this one is completely up to you, but the general advice is to not tell people before the first scan because things can sometimes go wrong and, if they do, the last thing you want is all of those people you told sending congratulations cards and asking you all about it. But of course a lot of people will still want to tell those closest to them earlier than this.

When you do tell loved ones your news, there can sometimes be a gap between the reaction you expect them to have and the reaction they actually have. Without even realizing it, I bet you have a version of the scene in your head of when you tell your mum or nana or best mate. And if they don't react that way, it can be surprising, confusing or upsetting. Maybe they won't be as happy as you'd hoped, maybe they'll cry, maybe they will give a simple 'oh dear'. But that just isn't something you can control. Try not to pin too much on this moment. You'll have a much more accurate read on how they feel a couple of years in and all will be a distant memory (that you might hold against them forever).

When (and if) you decide the time is right to announce your news to the rest of the world, a convenient thing to do these days is the social media post. It's an easy way to tell lots of people at once and it keeps all of the discussion and reaction in one place so you don't need to answer the same questions from everyone. It's also your chance to get the biggest likes-haul you've ever had, unless you've had a photo with Mike Tyson.

There are different styles you can employ for this announcement and you've probably seen a few of them. Some people post pictures of scans next to a cinema board announcing 'Baby Lewis coming next June'; some post black-and-white photos of anonymous babies' feet with a phrase on it like 'our family is about to get two feet bigger'; some mums pose wearing funny T-shirts, like one with the words 'ICE ICE' above where the baby will be. I've even seen a picture of a dog wearing a T-shirt that says 'I'm going to be a brother', which raised a hell of a lot of questions in my head.

11

You might think some of these styles are absolutely lovely and some of them are the most cringeworthy things you'll ever see, but try not to judge these parents – it's an emotional time and it's a hard thing to know how to announce. They won't judge you either. Unless you do that dog thing.

ANDY PARSONS: If a mate of mine told me he was about to become a dad, I'd be incredibly positive about it; there's no point telling them all the shit that goes with it – you may as well be happy beforehand because it is about to be a massive arse-ache for 18 years and quite possibly forever. Because that's the thing about parenting... everything else in your life may be temporary – your job, your relationship, even your nationality – but you are about to be a parent for life. And you can kid yourself that your kids will be different – that they won't be the selfish, ungrateful, difficult, moaning, time-sapping, holiday-wrecking money pit that you were – but they won't. You might convince yourself that having a second kid will make having the first easier because they will have somebody else to play with, whereas in fact it will just be double the shit. You could kid yourself that average UK happiness steadily increases from late forties onwards because jobs get easier or people understand themselves better, whereas in truth it's because of all the increased happiness of parents whose kids have finally left home.

If you did tell your mate all the huge list of negatives, they might say, 'I only said I was having a kid but you're crapping on about it endlessly like it's the only thing you're able to talk about', and you could say, 'Ah, that's another thing I should mention...'

Telling work

Even though you'll have to tell the company you work for at some point to give them a heads-up you'll be taking paternity leave, it's a lot less of a big deal for men than it is for women. Unfairly for them, their pregnancy announcement can often come with a negative impact on their career and they might find they get treated differently from the moment they share their news. In contrast, it's been shown that men's careers improve after having children. Yet another bit of proof that life is a lot easier for men. Look down between your legs right now and say 'thanks again, little guy.'

Your announcement isn't going to send your boss into a spin because it will be assumed you're only going to take a couple of weeks off. Two weeks is the standard paternity leave a father is entitled to in the UK, although more and more companies are becoming flexible on this, offering longer leave and the option for shared parental leave. Shared parental leave means the mum takes less than her entitled maternity (at the time of writing, in the UK, this is up to 39 weeks' statutory paid leave and up to 52 weeks off) and you take more. So, in theory, she could go back to work after a few weeks and you could be at home for months. But this is a fairly recent development and far from the norm.

There's no rush for you to tell other people at work either because, as soon as you do, it will be the theme of your small talk every single day for months. So if I were you, I'd wait until you are really sick of the chat about the weather or the faulty microwave and then – and only then – deploy your brand-new chat subject. From that point onwards, you'll have the following exchange each time you get in a lift:

'How long have you got left?'

'A few months.'

'Get your sleep in now!' [Polite half laugh which lasts for as long as possible, then awkward silence for the rest of the lift journey.]

SCANS

The ultrasound scans are both incredibly exciting and worrying. You are offered two during the pregnancy (sometimes more if they want to monitor you for any reason). The first is between 8 and 14 weeks and the second is between 18 and 21 weeks. The first scan is sometimes called the dating scan and it gives you a due date. It's worth mentioning that this date is *very* rough and your baby can be born weeks and weeks either side. But getting this date also means you can do the maths and pinpoint which particular romantic evening got her pregnant. This is when your eyes will widen and you'll go, 'Oh, it was *that* time', then you agree to pretend it was the lovely night with all the candles and not the drunken fumble that you threw up after.

It's at this scan when you actually see your baby (or babies!) for the first time, and it is confirmed that you weren't imagining the whole thing. For some dads, this is a really magical moment and they will burst into tears at the sight of their baby. For some, the feeling will be one of terror because the whole thing suddenly gets real. Some dads won't feel anything. But none of these reactions are wrong or right and they don't have any bearing on the type of dad you will go on to be.

For me, it was a huge feeling of relief when I first saw my baby. I was content, but I certainly wasn't overcome with emotion and I had no urge to cry. After a few minutes, the relief settled and I just got sleepy. I didn't realize how long you have to sit in a dark room. It seemed to take ages and, as lovely as it is to see your baby, it's just an undetailed blob when you stop concentrating, so after a short while, it's easy to drift off.

When the checks are complete, they will offer you a picture of the scan of your baby to take away, and it usually costs a few quid so take some cash. Well, they say it's your baby, but it would be a very easy scam for them to just print off the same picture for everyone. They all look the same at this point. I'm not saying that's what they do, but they could.

As well as the lovely little moments watching your baby wriggle around, there's a more serious side. You will also be offered screenings to assess the chances your baby has Down's, Edwards' and Patau's syndromes at the first scan. You don't have to have them, but most people do. This screening doesn't come with any risk, but it also won't tell you for certain if your baby has one of these conditions, just if the probability is high, and you get the result in the post a while later. I have to warn you that when you know that this is what they're testing for it is hard not to play out hypothetical situations in your head. You will likely have moral dilemmas about what you would do if your baby is shown to have one of the conditions. You'll possibly ask yourself really difficult questions about whether you'd be able to cope and it might throw you into a place of guilt or even upsetting disagreements with your partner. Or you might avoid discussing it at all because you're worried about what your partner might say or you're worried about what your partner might think about what you say.

Out of all the things you will worry about during the pregnancy, this one is not worth the mental discomfort it will cause you. The likelihood of Down's syndrome, for instance, is very low at around 1 in 700 (with a higher likelihood in older mums). And it's hard to really know how you would feel about something like this until it actually happens. So, if you can, try not to spend too much time with that hypothetical.

If your results show a high probability, you might be offered further diagnostics tests, where they might take samples of the cells from the placenta or some of the amniotic fluid (the stuff that surrounds the baby in the womb) to analyze chromosomes. But these do come with the risk of miscarriage, albeit a very low one. This is a horrible dilemma to be in and there is a lot to think about. The NHS recommends the charity ARC (Antenatal Results and Choices), which offers loads of information about results and your choices.

It's also worth mentioning here that there is a new test called non-invasive prenatal testing (NIPT), which is currently being rolled out across the UK. It is done via a blood test taken from the mother and uses cutting-edge DNA technology to assess the likelihood of Down's, Edwards' and Patau's syndromes and poses no risk to mother or baby.

ELIS JAMES: I had never been anxious or nervous, but I found myself being far less relaxed about the whole thing than I had expected. We would go into scans and I'd see couples in the waiting room smiling at each other and holding hands, whereas I just felt like I was about to sit the most important exam of my life without having done any of the revision. Whenever I'd see a couple looking relaxed I'd think, 'Don't you get it? You're about to see a picture of your baby...on a screen! WHY AREN'T YOU CONSUMED BY WORRY?'

I also hadn't realized how easy a deal the man gets during the pregnancy. Isy would get so tired I would have to take her shoes off for her as soon as she entered the house, and she found it difficult to sleep, especially during the last few months. It felt very unfair.

Finding out the sex

Usually during your second scan you'll get the option to find out the gender of your baby. But the main purpose of the scan is to look at your baby's development in detail and check for physical abnormalities, and I certainly remember feeling like any talk of gender was seen as trivial by our sonographer. This is a bit unfair because it is something every parent is thinking about. There are benefits to both finding out and keeping it a surprise. Some people say finding out helps them bond with the baby before it's born and means you can plan things a bit better. But if you choose to wait it keeps the excitement, and I know my wife found it was an extra little thing to help her through the difficult parts of labour. I can imagine it's the same feeling I have when watching *Midsomer Murders* – it's a real struggle and there are points when I just feel like giving up, but I have to see it through to the end to find out who it is. Waiting until the baby arrives to find out also gives you the perfect line to use when out shopping: 'Do you really think we should spend all that money on clothes/a pillow/blah blah blah before we even know the gender?'

To be honest, they are both pretty great and exciting options and the choice will probably depend on your and your partner's personalities. It's worth noting they can't be 100 per cent certain of your baby's gender because babies aren't always in the best position for you to see and everything is still pretty small. No offence to your unborn baby, but their penis, if they have one, is tiny.

CHANGES FOR HER AND YOU

The changes for a pregnant woman are monumental. There are the obvious physical ones. She may be sick for months on end. She's growing in size and weight every single day and getting more and more uncomfortable as she does. Her organs are getting squished and she'll become short of breath because her lungs have no room to inflate. Her back will ache with the weight, which gets greater every day. She is constantly knackered, but can't sleep because every time she tries the little human lying inside her starts wriggling around. Then there are the mental changes.

She's feeling the pressure to do everything possible to grow her baby the best she can. Dealing with the constant worry she will do the wrong thing or eat the wrong thing or something bad will happen for no reason. She has the feeling of watching her body change in ways she might not like. The sense that she isn't herself anymore and has become just a vessel. The constant anxiety over the birth, which can seem scary and impossible. Her hormones will be all over the place too and she'll go from rage to happiness to heartbreak within seconds for no reason.

Compared to all this, your changes are almost not worth mentioning. You lucky bastard. But there are thousands of books for pregnant women. So, now we've acknowledged and agreed how much harder it is for them, let's indulge ourselves. This is a book for dads (and mums are unlikely to be reading this bit) so we can afford to feel sorry for ourselves about the things we go through.

For a lot of men, it comes as a surprise how little changes for you at first because there are zero physical changes, unless you are one of the men who experiences 'sympathy weight gain'. I know, that sounds like an excuse, but it's a pretty good one ('Yes, I've developed a beer gut, but it's because I'm feeling *your* pain.')

You don't really have to alter your behaviour in any way either. But for men, the first big changes are psychological ones and they will come gradually or hit you all at once at another time (more on that later). As a man – maybe because of traditional gender roles or stuff we've experienced in our own families – there are certain pressures we feel or put on ourselves. Many of you will be worried about providing for your family financially, protecting them, and you're probably worried you're going to have to change things about yourself and your lifestyle that you don't really want to change.

There are bound to be moments when you freak out and think you're not ready to become a dad yet. But the truth is, if you waited to feel 100 per cent ready, you'd be waiting forever. There are always things you still want to do before you get 'tied down' and you will probably always be scared of growing up and having more responsibilities. But being a dad doesn't signal the end of everything. It's the beginning of a brand-new thing. Yes, some stuff will change and get harder, but you'll still be able to do all the things you enjoy, you just might have to plan some of them in advance or build up considerably more credit with your other half than you used to. But the flipside is that there are so many more interesting and exciting adventures about to open up to you.

Your life isn't over when you become a dad. Just look at someone like Liam Gallagher. He's a dad; does his life look like it's over? And most men worry they can't do it. But like I said, Liam Gallagher.

IAIN STIRLING: I thought about my own behaviour a lot more during the pregnancy – mainly what effect my behaviour will have on those around me. I imagined if someone behaved like that towards my child and how that would make me feel. I'm a better person for it – considerably more anxious, but better.

HOW MUCH DOES A BABY COST?

A shitload. But don't worry, that's over the course of a lifetime and anything costs a staggering amount when you work it out like that. You'd probably be floored by the amount you will spend on plastic bags over your lifetime and they're not going to surround you and comfort you on your death bed. Unless things get really bad.

It's obviously best to start budgeting early and save up as much as you can before the birth. But as long as you're doing what you can, try not to get too worried about money. Babies don't arrive with an invoice that has to be paid immediately. The costs early on can actually be really low because they don't need a lot at first (see page 39 for a list of the essentials).

But in a section like this, you probably want an actual figure. There have been plenty of studies on this and they vary by the tens (and even hundreds) of thousands. That could be because most are carried out by businesses with a vested interest. Be as sceptical of these as you would of a pie manufacturer's survey that shows women love a man who smells of steak and kidney. Businesses know that if they manage to normalize spending huge amounts on baby products then people are more likely to spend huge amounts on their baby products.

But figures like this can be terrifying for parents who don't have much money. Across the country, and across the world, people are making it work with wildly different budgets. You can spend a fortune on the latest, most stylish stuff or you can be a bit more resourceful and buy second-hand or even get stuff for free.

A more trusted source than the baby company-funded

surveys is The Child Poverty Action Group, whose latest report says that the cost of raising a child until the age of 18 (including rent and childcare) is £151,000 for couples and £185,000 for lone parents (presumably because they need more childcare and rent isn't as good value for a single person). There's no doubt it's an eye-watering figure but, as I say, it doesn't come all at once and, thankfully, we live in a country that provides some financial help to parents who need it, even though the government could be doing a lot more. A quick search for 'benefits for new parents' will tell you what you're entitled to and most people get at least a small amount.

That large overall figure also doesn't take into account all of the money you save as a parent because of lifestyle changes. You're probably starting to realize that you'll no longer be going on as many boozy weekends away or out for romantic meals in restaurants as much as you used to (sorry) so a lot of the cost of a child isn't extra, it's just reallocation of the money you'd spend anyway. And once you've got all of the essentials, the running costs can be really low. At first, it's just milk and nappies really. When they start to eat, they can usually have a bit of the thing you were making for yourself. Eventually they will start wanting things like cool toys and trainers, but by that point you can probably get them to take on a paper round to pay their way.

The most important thing to remember is the love that you give your child will far outweigh anything that money could ever provide. As long as they are cared for, fed and kept warm, I doubt they really know the difference between living in a single-bedroom flat and living in Simon Cowell's mansion (except for the guy wandering around in high-waisted trousers, crushing dreams). But there's no doubt it still takes a little while to adjust. Especially to the feeling that, from the moment your baby arrives, your money is no longer yours, it's your family's. That's nice in some ways. It's good to have something this important to work for and you will probably make more sensible financial decisions now because they are for the good of your family.

But another side effect is the guilt you now feel for anything you buy that is for you. Getting yourself a pair of trainers or a haircut feels selfish. Each time you pay over the odds for a craft beer, you'll feel like you are drinking away your child's milk money. Again, it'll settle down after a while. In the meantime, you can make yourself feel better by growing your hair a bit longer, wearing holes in your trainers and drinking cooking wine.

Child benefit

Unless you or your partner earn over £50k you'll get just over £20 a week for your first child. And it's easy to claim at gov.uk. If you do earn over £50k, you'll still get it, but you'll be taxed on it, so it won't be as much. And if you earn over £60k, then pleased to meet you, Mr Alan Sugar. You lose all of it in tax at this point, sorry.

THE BUMP

One side effect of pregnancy you might have noticed if you're eagle-eyed is the growth of a rather large thing in roughly the centre of your partner. It starts as a little bump and, within a few months, swells to a size that defies physics. If you were to draw an accurate picture of a pregnant woman, it'd look like you're really quite crap at drawing. I'm not sure how they don't all just topple over.

The general things a woman needs to do to care for the bump are the same things she needs to do to care for herself: eat well, rest and exercise where possible. But she'll also be knackered, her moods will be all over the place and she'll get weird cravings. So, while you should support her healthy lifestyle by cooking and joining her on walks, she'll already feel like her body isn't her own, so I wouldn't pass comment on what she is or isn't putting in it if I were you, unless one of her cravings is cigars. Even then, you risk her taking it from her mouth and putting it out on your arm while she says, 'You grow the fucking baby then.'

Sounds

Your baby can hear stuff long before it's born so, presuming you talk to your partner, it will get used to your voice, then find it a comfort when it is out in the real world. This means that, as stupid as it will feel, it absolutely makes sense to talk to the bump. It helps to start to form a bond with your baby, and your partner will quite possibly find it adorable. The baby may even communicate back with kicks, which will give you a lovely feeling of connection and it has the bonus effect of being a funny way to mess with the mum. It's like she's wearing those trick electrical buzzers, but the remote is your voice and the buzzer is a human in her belly.

It's also worth remembering this sound recognition when picking which TV programmes to watch during the pregnancy, because new research shows that babies can understand sounds well enough when in the womb to retain memory of them after the birth. After our baby was born, he seemed to be comforted every time he heard the *Friends* theme tune, which is what my wife watched constantly during pregnancy. With that in mind, choose something you're happy to stick on regularly when the baby is here. I'm very grateful we made our way through *Game of Thrones* before my wife got pregnant. I loved it, but I'm not sure how I'd have felt about having a baby who can only sleep to the murderous screams of the Dothraki warriors.

Kicking

There comes a point where you start to feel – and later see – the baby moving within your wife's abdomen. Some dads will find this magical and some (more normal) dads will find it strange to see a human squirming around inside another human. But you do get used to it and seeing your child moving becomes as reassuring as it is weird.

Oh, and here's something to watch out for as the bump grows: if she has an inny belly button, it can pop out (not across the room, just to an 'outy' position). So that's a little bit of fun for you. It usually goes back after birth.

Things to say and not say

It can be confusing at first because it seems like the rules have changed and it's now acceptable to talk about a pregnant woman's size. But be careful, my friend, because it's all in the detail. When you are talking about her being big (which will inevitably happen, so it is weird not to talk about it) always direct your observations at the bump. Saying 'the bump is huge!' is totally fine and even shows just how much you appreciate what she's going through. But if you find yourself saying 'you are huge!' you are on very dodgy ground.

Some other more complimentary things to say are to tell her how neat the bump is or how she doesn't look pregnant from behind. But only say these if they are true. If she's put on eight stone it will sound sarcastic and she might look at you like she wants to throw a vase at your head. Or she might just throw a vase at your head.

The baby's movements

As the pregnancy progresses, the mum will feel movements. It begins with gentle fluttering, usually between 16 and 24 weeks, then eventually becomes more noticeable kicks and wriggles. While this can get uncomfortable and annoying for the mum, it is comforting to feel.

There is no set amount of times a baby should move in a day, but a woman will get used to her baby's habits. So, when they change and the baby goes quiet, it can send you both into a panicked and spiralling negative thought pattern. Like when you phone your partner and they don't answer a couple of times so you convince yourself they have driven off a cliff and you have to start planning your life without them.

But – and I speak from personal experience here – there can be loads of reasons you might not feel the baby moving. It might've shifted positions, making movements less noticeable. It might be surrounded by a lot of fluid. It might just be having a lazy day. So you need to avoid jumping to the worst conclusions every time and set about doing something to alleviate the worry.

First of all, if your partner ever feels that something is wrong, you can always contact the hospital. They will likely ask you to pop in so they can check everything over. Don't worry about doing this – they will be more than happy to put your mind at ease and they have people coming in all day every day for this exact reason. I don't know anyone who hasn't done this at least once during the pregnancy. There are a couple of quick fixes you can do at home too, to try to get the baby wriggling. The mum can drink a nice cold glass of orange juice or you can jiggle her belly about a bit (this is the only time you should EVER do this).

FIRST AID

There are a couple of things that were on my to-do list for years and years that always seemed easy to put off, but played on my mind because I knew that if I suddenly needed them, it'd be too late. One of these was to learn what to do if you get caught in sinking sand and another was to learn what do if someone is choking. Just before our baby was born we finally decided we needed to do a first aid course.

There are companies set up specifically to teach new and prospective parents first aid. They can come to your house and you can have several of your parent friends round and split the cost. I can't tell you what a reassurance it is to know what you need to do if a baby is choking, hits their head or cuts themselves, so I recommend booking one. I'm still not sure what you do in quicksand. It's either move around a lot or not at all. Hmmm.

CLEANING UP SHIT

If you've got a pet, it starts now! Cat faeces can carry a parasite that can harm unborn babies, so the litter tray is your job for the next few months I'm afraid, pal. But don't sulk too much; on balance you've probably still got the best deal. Beware of hamsters, mice, guinea pigs, snakes, lizards, turtles and other exotic pets too. They can all carry germs that can be harmful to pregnant women. Consider this job as practice, because when your baby comes along, cleaning up shit is going to become one of your biggest pastimes.

HAVING SEX

There is no telling how pregnancy will affect your partner's libido. Some pregnant women will be keener than ever. Some will take a nun-like vow of abstinence. Some will be filled with desire one moment, then repulsed by the thought of intimacy the next. In my experience, this seems to occur the moment I take my clothes off.

The way you feel about sex might change too. You'll almost certainly want to still have it because you're a man, but there will be more things on your mind than usual. Firstly, your partner has a baby bump. You're not sure whether you're meant to find this attractive or not, and whichever way you feel, it feels like the wrong one. If you're not attracted to this new shape, you'll feel guilty. How can you stop fancying your partner now she's having your kid, you pig?! And if you realize that pregnant women turn you on more than anything, you'll feel wrong in a different way and fret about the complications your new-found fetish will cause you in the future. Well, don't worry; if you're not mad on the bump look, it's OK – it only lasts a few months. And if you are, great! Enjoy it! If you need to, you can always have more babies after this one.

You'll also worry about your unborn baby when having sex. It feels awkward knowing your child is right there and most men are concerned they might poke it. Well, unless you're that bloke whose picture gets circulated around every single stag do WhatsApp group, you'll be fine. You're not going to get anywhere near. And, even if you are that bloke (hello mate, I never thought I'd get to talk to you), it's still not really a worry because the baby is in an amniotic sac (imagine a Zorb filled with liquid) and the cervix is closed, keeping the baby in…and you out. So, it couldn't be any more well-protected. Don't worry about your kid seeing your penis either. For the reasons already explained, it won't be able to, and even if it could, it has no concept of why seeing its dads would be so mortifyingly embarrassing.

The key thing to keep in mind is to pick positions which suit her new shape and avoid anything that involves you putting all of your body weight on her stomach. She'll feel conscious of her new body as well, so as long as you're aware of that (don't *keep* going on about how brilliant her new huge boobs are) there's no reason you shouldn't have loads of sex! (Apart from the usual ones: she has a headache, backache, she's tired, she preferred you when you were in better physical shape…)

In summary, while the changes that you experience as a dad throughout the bulk of the pregnancy are nothing compared to those of the mum, they still involve bigger mental shifts than you will have experienced in a long time. In the first six or seven months, the changes will be slow and hard to pin down, but as you enter the final couple of months before the birth, things start to ramp up...

CHAPTER 2

THE BUILD-UP

Once you've managed to get your head around the fact that you are going to be a dad, a new feeling is likely to take over – the feeling that you aren't ready and you will never be ready. Well, you're right, you aren't, but don't worry because you're not meant to be yet. In this chapter we'll discuss all of the things you need to do. But relax because it is all very manageable and you've still got quite a while before there are any huge changes to your life.

ANTENATAL CLASSES

Antenatal or NCT classes are optional sessions you can do, usually at around eight to ten weeks before your due date, to prepare you for the birth and the first important parts of parenthood, like how to feed your baby.

After going along to the classes, parents will often come up with a 'birth plan', which is a blueprint for the way you want things done and includes stuff like where you want to give birth, how you want to give birth and the amount of drugs you do or don't want.

But one of the main reasons people go to the classes is to meet and discuss things with other people who are also about to have a baby. It can be very reassuring to have other people who are in the same boat as you, and often you'll all join a WhatsApp group, which can be a great place to ask questions, share worries and establish yourself as the guy who always posts the funniest memes.

We didn't do any of this, though. Through a mixture of poor organization, moving to a new part of the country three weeks before the birth and a fear of having to make new friends, we didn't go to the classes. I regretted it a little bit at the birth when I didn't know what the hell was going on. Luckily some of my mates did do them, so I'll hand over to them to share their experiences.

KERRY GODLIMAN: My husband and I did the NCT course, but all the science stuff is Google-able, to be honest. I mainly joined it to make friends. It felt good to have a little crew of local people going through the same thing at the same time. I did drag my husband to a birth rehearsal workshop. That nearly split us up, as he trod on the 'newborn baby' doll and kept saying 'good girl' to me through the breathing exercises. I just wanted to punch him in the face.

ELIS JAMES: Shamefully, I think I was slightly in denial and didn't take the classes very seriously, although we did make some really good friends which was invaluable, especially during the early months. For months we sat in a church hall and I gently took the piss, and then three months later I was in tears, wishing I'd listened. It was like my A-levels all over again.

IAIN STIRLING: We had a couple of one-on-one sessions with a midwife, which was great. She taught us the basics but also that you shouldn't change everything you do as the baby will need to fit into your own lifestyle. How practical that is is very much up for debate, but it's a lovely idea right!?

THE HOSPITAL TOUR

Whether you are going private or with the NHS, you will be offered a hospital tour so you can familiarize yourself with the place and ask questions about what everything is and what will happen on the day. Of all of the tours you'll do in your life, the hospital tour will be the least entertaining. Unless, like me, you've done the open-top bus tour of Rhyl.

It feels more like the 'open house' estate agents do when they show you around at the same time as a load of other people. Except this particular house is really depressing and you don't want to buy it and the estate agent couldn't give a shit if you do. But you will anyway because all of the other houses are exactly the same.

You – and several couples who all look like slightly different versions of you – will shuffle from one room to another and gawp at stuff that it's almost impossible to have an opinion on ('These are the beds. That's a chair. That's a machine with a name you don't understand.') and you will just nod along.

There might be some couples who've got kids already. And they might have brought them on the tour. Because they might be idiots. Like the ghosts that visit Scrooge in the night, they are here to show you what your future could be like if you're not careful. There was a young boy on our tour who constantly shouted 'Anus!' as the midwife tried to tell everyone about what happens in an emergency. His parents just looked defeated, like they had stopped trying to explain to him why you just can't go about your life shouting 'Anus' all the time. I remember thinking 'God, I hate kids.' Then I realized what I'd done.

If it's a nice hospital, they might have 'birthing suites' with pools, inflatable balls and colourful lights. These are clearly the best places to give birth in but, to be honest with you, your partner will give birth in whichever room is free and in whatever way is best for her and the baby on the day. And it probably won't be the nicest birthing room because that's the one they are giving a tour in and a young boy is in there, shouting 'Anus!'

The only things you really need to focus on are that the place looks clean enough, you can get there easily when she goes into labour, what to do when you get there (where to go, how things are different if you arrive in the middle of the night and the doors are locked, where to park that won't cripple you financially, etc.) and the staff don't look like monsters. If you do feel really unhappy with the hospital, then the good thing is you can just go and look at another one. But then you'll have to go through the ordeal of another tour, which you probably won't want to do. Welcome to the world of compromises. Get comfortable.

EXPECTATIONS VERSUS REALITY

Maybe you've got yourself a nice, neat birth plan so you feel like you know exactly how the birth is going to go: it will happen in a pool and there will be music and mood lighting and everything will be lovely. I hope that's the case, but try showing your birth plan to the two women who are already using the two hospital pools when you arrive, and you'll soon realize it isn't worth the paper it's written on. The midwives will certainly try to do things according to your wishes, but of all of the people I've spoken to, none have stuck completely to their birth plan. So, just prepare yourselves that the birthing room you wanted might be busy, the meditation sounds playlist might not load and your partner, who was dead set on a hypnobirth, might decide at the last minute that what she'd really love is lots and lots of drugs. But I assure you, you won't care about any of this. Everyone is going to do the best thing for your little baby, regardless of the plan.

MATTHEW CROSBY: By the time we were finally allowed into our own delivery room my wife and I had been awake for over 24 hours. She lay on a bed, attached to a variety of medical apparatus, and I was given use of a large, semi-reclinable chair; the NHS version of what Joey and Chandler would watch *Baywatch* in. About fifteen minutes later, my wife's blood pressure suddenly dropped and the midwife pulled the red emergency cord, filling the tiny room with about nine or ten doctors and nurses. There was a frantic rush as they worked together to right the situation and, for a brief moment, it was all a bit scary for my wife. I say, 'for my wife' as I wasn't technically present for this bit. The second my body had connected with that reclining chair I'd fallen asleep. Even the alarm and the mad scramble of medical practitioners hadn't woken me up. At one point during the scrum, one of the doctors asked my wife, 'Is that your partner?', she confirmed that it was and he responded with, 'He's very good at sleeping.'

It's a dubious badge of honour I wear to this day. I may not be good at much, but I am medically proficient at being asleep.

It's worth noting that, since writing this, I have been informed by my wife that I actually hadn't been awake for 24 hours. She had, but I'd managed to find several opportunities to get my head down during our first few hours in hospital. Like I say, it's a talent.

Our best-laid birthing plan of 'no interventions' and 'hypnobirthing techniques' had gone out of the window, but we still wanted to make the room as comfortable and cosy as we could. My wife played her *Harry Potter* audiobook through the Bluetooth speakers we'd borrowed from my dad and I grabbed the battery-operated fairy lights I'd bought off the internet. Opening the box, I pulled out a string of tree lights that would have struggled to cover a bonsai. They must have been 10cm long. To be honest, I had wondered why they were 99p.

BABY LOSS

Sadly, some people will experience the heartbreak of miscarriage (losing a baby before 24 weeks) or stillbirth (losing a baby after 24 weeks) and you might be shocked by just how common it is. In the UK, it is estimated that one in four pregnancies end in miscarriage.

Most miscarriages happen within the first 12 weeks and thankfully the risk greatly reduces after this point. According to one study, once a pregnancy gets past six or seven weeks and the embryo has a heartbeat, the risk of miscarriage drops to 10 per cent.

When you lose your baby during pregnancy, it is hard to find any comfort. But there is a lot of hope. The overwhelming amount of women who miscarry can still go on to have healthy pregnancies and children. Even women who have multiple miscarriages still have a good chance of a successful pregnancy.

If the cause is unknown, six out of ten women who have had three miscarriages will go on to have a healthy baby.

Tommy's is a charity working to research and reduce baby loss. They also offer a lot of support and information on their website: tommys.org.

BUYING STUFF

In this brand-new situation, where you have no idea what is to come, you will feel underprepared, because you're not quite sure what you are preparing for. So, you'll try to relieve this anxiety by doing something you know how to do: buy a load of shit. The baby world is full of the type of gadgets that a lot of blokes find irresistible (the manufacturers know exactly what they are doing) so it's pretty easy to feel the need to buy *everything*. It means you can go to bed at night and think, 'I must be prepared for fatherhood because I read a hundred Amazon reviews today.' If this makes you feel more relaxed, then that's fine.

But…you should expect a different buying process to usual. You'll find that, because the stakes are so much higher and there's more emotion involved, even the reviews are different. It feels like everyone has much more extreme views on the product and it's not uncommon to see a review that says, 'This product saved our lives!' directly above a review for the same product that says, 'This product ruined our lives!' You wouldn't think people could feel so strongly about breast pads and musical clouds. You'll spend ages weighing up options, always feeling guilty for even considering choosing the cheaper one, because it feels like you are putting money before the well-being of your unborn child. But that's how the baby industry works. They know exactly what pressures you are feeling and they will do their best to make you feel them more, so it's no surprise you then get stressed out by how much it all will be.

Hopefully I can relieve some of this worry by telling you that you really don't need to get everything yet because a baby's needs are very modest at the start and, worst-case scenario, if you realize you haven't got something you need, we live in a day and age where you can order something from your phone and have it at your front door in a matter of hours.

Here are the essentials and a few optional bits as well:

Babygrows, vests, hats, bibs and socks

These are your bread and butter. The baby will get through a lot of these each day, so you need plenty in rotation. The multipacks you get in most supermarkets are as good as anything. Try to get the vests with the 'envelope'-style neck. They widen to twice the size of normal ones, so they are much easier to put over the soft, delicate head of your new baby. You can even put them on and take them off from the bottom of your baby and so avoid their squishy head altogether. This function really comes into its own when your baby craps everywhere and you can just take it off over their legs instead of their face and hair like you had to with all of the poor little babies in the past.

Babygrows use press studs so, in theory, they should be easy to put on. But in practice, the new dad trying to learn how a baby-grow works feels like a dog trying to learn how to rewire a plug.

You should go for more than one size at first, because even though the medical professionals will predict how big your baby is going to be, no one really knows until it is born. And if you do have a surprisingly big baby, everyone will be talking about its weight constantly, so it'll be self-conscious enough without you making it look like an overstuffed sausage by forcing it into an outfit two sizes too small.

Muslins

These are big, soft, thin bits of material you can use for everything from cleaning the baby, to wrapping them up, to putting on your shoulder to protect it from all the puke. You'll get through a load of these and you'll wonder why everything isn't made out of this amazing stuff, whatever it is. Remember to wash them with fabric conditioner or they will come out feeling like a giant poppadum and your partner will look at you like you're a dickhead.

Nappies (plus baby wipes, cream, nappy bags and a changing mat)

Get a load of this stuff in. Over time, you'll find out which nappies you like best, but often it will just depend on how well they fit your baby. So better to start with Aldi's own brand and, if you don't like them, gradually work your way up to Pampers, getting more annoyed with each jump in cost.

You can also get more eco-friendly alternatives than ever before and there are non-disposable nappies that are cheaper in the long run, better for the world your kid is going to grow up in and surprisingly low-hassle.

Nappy bags and changing mats are all pretty similar and I'd recommend Sudocrem to keep your baby's bum soft and stop it getting sore.

A lot of parents will buy changing tables as well. These are usually built with a set of drawers and mean you can change your baby much higher up, saving your back and knees from a little bit (but by no means all) of the damage fatherhood will cause.

Breast pump

If your baby is breastfeeding, you might need one of these. When your partner first uses it, it will probably make her feel nervous and self-conscious because it looks like a contraption you'd use on a dairy farm. But it doesn't hurt or anything. The breast pump means the mum can relieve any pressure in her boobs and store up breast milk to use later or let you feed your baby with it from a bottle.

Unless you've got a super-high-tech one, the noise is a lot louder than you'd expect, but this will soon become normal. The repetitive pumping and releasing of the suction cup is about to become the soundtrack to your life. It's one of those sounds that will become lodged in your mind forever and years from now will transport you back to these early stages of fatherhood, in the same way the sound of a dial-up modem takes you back to MSN chat rooms and slow-loading porn.

Bottles (and formula, if needed)

We'll discuss breast versus bottle later (see page 101), but even if the baby is breastfeeding, there could be times when Mum expresses milk to give the baby milk from a bottle, so you might still need them. They are available everywhere and the teats come in different sizes (as the baby gets older, the hole gets bigger to let more milk through). There are a lot of brands, and I assume they must all be good enough, otherwise they'd have gone bust. So, just have a browse and pick the ones you like the look of.

With formula, certain ones can cause more wind in babies than others, but it depends on the baby. So, the best thing to do is try it with your baby and, if they like it, great. If I were you I'd start off with the ones that are most easily available because you'll be constantly running out and having to nip out for more.

A lot of the powders are also available ready-made. These are great to have for when you're on the go, are in a rush or just can't be arsed mixing stuff, but they cost a lot more and you'd have to buy hundreds of the bottles to keep you going.

Moses basket or crib

Not much to say about these. Moses baskets are baskets. I think they are named after the lad from the Bible and are perfect for carrying your sleeping baby around the house and, presumably, if the need arises, for floating them along the Nile to safety.

Or you can get a crib if Moses baskets feel a bit old-fashioned and you're not planning on carrying your baby around all over the place. Cribs are a bit sturdier too. There are also more modern versions you can connect to the side of your bed, so that the baby can sleep closely to you or your partner and you can check on them in the middle of the night without having to get up.

Whether you choose a Moses basket or crib, they will need little mattresses (they often come included) and a few bedsheets so you've got spares, because babies can be a bit messy.

Blankets

You'll need some blankets to wrap your baby up in to keep them warm and many these days are 'anti-suffocation', which will put your mind at ease. Knowing exactly what you should and shouldn't put in the crib or cot is a source of confusion and anxiety for a lot of parents, so take a look at page 115 for a really clear guide from Dr Adam Kay.

Baby monitor

You can spend a painfully long amount of time comparing these, but as someone who has – through a mixture of breaking them, losing them and having multiple children – tried loads of them, I can tell you they are all very similar, many of them even using the exact same software, so the only difference in a lot of cases is the shape.

Most come with a screen now, so even the basic ones are much more advanced than the audio-only ones everyone used in the past. The ones with screens are much more fun to play with too. I once saw a guy on the internet set his up by the oven to watch his pizza cook.

Pram

It's unlikely you'll have a huge amount of influence on what pram you get. It's like wedding planning – you are allowed an opinion, but if it's not the right one first time, she'll patiently wait until it is. My wife already had an eye on the pram she wanted, way before she gave birth or met me.

It did look really nice, but, practically speaking, it was absolute shite. It seems like they spent months thinking about the detail of the trim and around three minutes on the wheels. They constantly felt like they were about to snap and were too far underneath the pram, so when you hit a curb or a leaf at any speed, the whole thing tipped forward. If not for the straps, the baby would have been catapulted across the street.

I was complaining to a mate about it and he said, 'Oh yeah, I could've told you that.' He's a prick, you see. But this is the key to getting a good one. Ask all of your mates with prams about theirs, because you are going to be using it so often, the little annoyances will become a big part of your life. Your dad friends will be able to give you an honest review, unblinded by that gorgeous goddamn trim.

They don't need to be expensive either. The internet is full of people selling second-hand prams that are as good as new. And when we had a second baby, we bought a double pram, but for about a fifth of the price of the first because we thought we wouldn't use it as much. It is ten times better than the designer one.

One of the biggest concerns you should have with your pram is how easy it is to get it into your front door and how much room it will take up in your entrance or hallway. Some of the lighter buggy-style ones may seem a bit less luxurious and stylish, but it's more than made up for when you have the smug feeling of being able to glide into your front door with ease and collapse it with ONE HAND. Always make sure to take the baby out before collapsing it though because it's much trickier to do so afterwards.

A note on cup holders

These are a nice idea, but are utterly useless. The whole concept is flawed. The moment you start pushing your pram along a surface that isn't completely flat, it rattles around like an egg cup attached to a pneumatic drill, sending hot coffee all over your jacket, shoes and baby. Unless your drink is in an airtight flask or you're planning on strolling around on a snooker table, it's futile. You'll have to pull over safely to enjoy your coffee properly or just hold it in your hand and guide the pram one-handed (fine on straight roads, but corners are tough).

Car seat

Even if you don't have a car, I've heard some hospitals say you have to have a car seat or they won't let you take your baby home from hospital as a safety measure. It's a rule that leaves them open to opportunistic parents, exploiting it to get free childcare for life. Just pop in and visit your baby whenever you like, but pretend you keep forgetting that bloomin' car seat.

But unless you're going to do this, you need to get one and there are new rules on car seats that say your kid has to have one from birth until they are 135cm tall or 12 years old, whichever is first. This means two things: Firstly, it's worth choosing one that will last. There are some great options that can be adjusted to accommodate a huge portion of this period and you just lose parts of it as the baby grows, like a rocket when going to the moon. Secondly, make sure your kid drinks lots of milk so they grow big and strong, because if they are still using a car seat when they go to secondary school, everyone will call them a 'car-seat wanker'.

You often end up with the same brand car seat as your pram, because they connect together. This meant our car seat was as complete shite as our pram. I know I could have returned it, but I thought it was easier to just let it piss me off every day for two years.

DAD TRICK Practise doing the buckle on each car seat you're considering buying and pick the easiest one. This will be something you have to do a million times, sometimes in pouring rain, sometimes with a crying kid and always in a rush, so you'll really appreciate it if it isn't too tricky.

Fitting the car seat

Maybe it's the mixture of materials – the hard plastic seat and the soft, limp seatbelt. Maybe it's the way the belt will retract back into a hole the moment you loosen your grip. Maybe it's the fact that, in a design error, most humans were only born with two hands. Maybe it's the pressure you're feeling that this should be a very simple job for a new dad and, if you're struggling with this, what are you going to do when all the real fathering starts? Maybe it's the worry that, if you get this wrong, it will only be exposed when you bump into a lamp post and your kid flies past your head (and you can just picture the look on your partner's face if that happened). Whatever the reason, this job is way more difficult and time-consuming than you'd expect. So, set aside a good chunk of your afternoon, load up some YouTube tutorial videos on your phone to guide you through it, some sweets for little rewards along the way and just relax. You can do it. Maybe.

That's all of the essentials covered! Here are a few more things that aren't as vital, but I do recommend:

Milk prep equipment

This will really improve your day-to-day life. We went without when we had our first baby and the feeding process was this: when the baby was hungry, I'd go and boil the kettle, mix some formula with the boiling water, run the bottle under the cold tap for about five minutes until the milk was cool enough for the baby to drink and my hand was numb. Then, I'd dash into my baby who would be a wreck because he'd been waiting so long for his milk. And I wouldn't be able to hold the bottle to feed him because I still had no feeling in my hand.

Then, after the feed, we'd wash the bottle in the sink, put it in a big pan and boil it on the stove to sterilize it. Because of the amount of bottles that needed sterilizing, this pan was constantly boiling for about a year. Every time you opened the kitchen door, it looked like you were emerging on to the *Stars in Their Eyes* stage. Wallpaper was peeling off the walls, everything was damp, and we just thought that's what everyone had to put up with.

It was only when we happened to be at a friend's house while they were feeding that we saw there was another way. They had a machine that instantly prepared milk to the perfect temperature at the push of a button and they also had a sterilizer you put in the microwave (basically a plastic tub with a little bit of water in). The whole thing was done in a matter of minutes, with no stress, and their house didn't feel like the inside of a Turkish bath.

My wife and I looked at each other, both on the verge of tears. I'm not sure if we were overcome with happiness about how much our lives were about to improve or sadness for the many months we had lost.

Dummies

We had a vague idea that we shouldn't use dummies, but I wasn't really sure why, other than I knew a lot of people were against them and I'd heard something about them affecting the way kids' teeth grow. So, we avoided them for the first few weeks, but one night when the baby would not stop crying and we were desperate for sleep, we couldn't think of a convincing reason not to try one. And wow – it was like we'd found the standby button on our kid. The possibility of wonky teeth at some point in the distant future is not something you care about when you finally get peace after weeks without sleep. Get sleep now, get braces later. I've since researched it and as long as the kid doesn't keep the dummy for years, it's unlikely to affect the teeth. It might affect the way a child talks though, so when they do start saying words, you'll need to think about how you can get your child to lose it and we'll discuss this in the 'Ditching the Dummies' section on page 276.

Some babies won't be bothered about dummies and some prefer to suck their thumb. This works well because it is always there for them, but a thumb is usually much harder to remove than a dummy.

Baby bath

Your baby will need cleaning at some point. Baby baths these days are so much better than the ones you'll probably remember from when you were young. They are shaped in a way that supports the baby, so their lower body is submerged, but their head is above water and they don't slip down. It's one of those design developments that makes you look back on the way things used to be and think that bath designers of the past were absolute numbskulls for not thinking of it.

Get a soft baby sponge too and a little thermometer that tells you the correct temperature. It's amazing how many times my wife and I disagree about this. She will say a bath is too hot while I swear it's too cold, or vice versa. The thermometer doesn't pick slides; it has no agenda. Without emotion or bias, it will clearly state who is right (me) and who is wrong (her). (See page 138 for more on bath time and how to clean your baby.)

Baby carrier or sling

It's hard to decide if carriers are the greatest or the lamest things in the world. Partly because it's difficult to work out if the smile people give you when you wear them is one that says, 'That looks adorable' or 'That looks ridiculous, you should be embarrassed, mate.'

All I know is, when you first put one on, it feels like you have your freedom back. You can go off-road, up steps and through narrow gates. You can start living your pre-baby rock-and-roll lifestyle again (presuming the sort of wild stuff you got up to in your younger days included going through narrow gates). Not only that, you can hold things like your phone and a drink. But just try not to catch a reflection of yourself because it's the image you've seen a thousand times in comedy film posters to denote a man whose life is over because he's got a baby.

You'll really notice the weight on your front after a while too and you'll have to limit just how hard you go on that off-road terrain because you become dangerously top-heavy, unbalanced and now have a kid's head blocking your view of the ground. Wear the carrier for too long and your spine will look like a question mark, so it's worth getting one of the ones with a little foam ledge on the front for the kid to sit on. This transfers the weight from your shoulders to your hips. So instead of making your spine bend unnaturally, it makes your hips ache. Which is, marginally, better.

I dare say you'll be pretty achey when you get home and take it off, but it's probably best to keep your quibbles to yourself. It's quite hard for me to describe the look my wife gave me when I complained about the difficulty of carrying a baby around on my front for just under 40 minutes.

RICH HALL: Once you've overcome the initial shock and elation of impending fatherhood, it's time to get real. You'll feel a desire to run out and buy all kinds of emotionally charged stuff: fluffy toys, cute little outfits, dazzling wallpaper, pram detritus – none of which is going to register one iota with your haploid-diploid bundle of semi-coherence. What you need to be buying is batteries. AAs, AAAs and Ds. An arsenal of them. You are going to spend the next ten years of your life ransacking your own home for more of the damn things, so start stockpiling now.

Push present

I wasn't entirely sure if this was a real thing when I was told about it. I'm still not. But apparently you're supposed to buy the mother a present for after the birth. While it's quite likely you'll lament this as 'another one of these bloody commercial traditions invented by Clinton Cards', I assure you that by the end of the birth, you'd happily give her a necklace with one of your kidneys attached if she wanted it (she probably won't). It's worth getting her something nice, because, by God, she is going to deserve it.

The push present doesn't have to be expensive, just thoughtful. But if you can't think of anything thoughtful enough then I'm afraid it probably does have to be expensive.

PREPARING THE HOME

Once you've got all of the essential stuff, you should try to organize your home in a way that will make things easiest when the baby arrives, bearing in mind you're going to be based in your living area for the best part of the next few weeks. So, declutter, get everything clean and comfy and batch cook as many meals as you can fit in your freezer. I can't tell you how grateful you'll be that you did this.

What will likely happen is your partner will tidy everything up and come up with a new system for the home. She'll tell you all about it, but you won't really listen because you'll be thinking about a documentary you watched about Komodo dragons or something else that feels more interesting at the time. Then, when the baby arrives, she'll ask you to get a blanket, but you won't know where it is. So, you'll try to distract her by telling her that Komodo dragons can weigh up to 14 stone. But it won't work and it will just piss her off. So, if you're not actually going to do any of the organizing yourself, at least try to pay attention when she tells you where stuff is.

You should also make sure you have working smoke alarms. It's a job most of us rarely do, but now is the time. It will keep your new baby safe and it's a proper dad job, so it'll give you a taste of things to come.

Oh, and you are going to need way more space than you ever thought, so if there are any ornaments, furniture or family members you could do without, get rid now.

MATTHEW CROSBY: We spent most of my daughter's early life in a small one-bedroom flat in Penge. My enduring memory of that time is the mornings. Despite what the estate agents were telling potential buyers, it really was a one-bedroom flat. My daughter was one and still sleeping in a cot at the foot of our bed. She'd begin each day by standing up and pointing at us ominously, like Donald Sutherland in *Invasion of the Body Snatchers*. I remember once attempting to comfort her back to sleep only using my left foot (the body part, not the moving Daniel Day-Lewis film) while simultaneously trying to keep the rest of my body asleep. Amazingly, neither part of my plan worked.

During this period she began learning to walk with the aid of a Winnie-the-Pooh stroller (and the unfailing love and support of her two wonderful parents). However, the living room was such a size that it was tricky for her to get any momentum. She'd take a step and a half and the stroller would meet a roadblock like the sofa or my ankle. So I'd have to pick her and the stroller up, turn them both 180 degrees, and then watch as she made a similarly brief journey back the other way. She must have done at least 100 laps of our front room in the space of just a few weeks. If only she'd used this activity as a money-raising exercise for the NHS, she'd have had a knighthood by now.

WHAT ARE YOU GOING TO CALL IT?

Choosing a baby name is easy. You just need to pick a classic one that is completely original, that hasn't just come back 'in' and hasn't just gone 'out', that everyone likes, but no one else has got, that isn't the name of someone famous or someone you know, and that isn't so strong your kid will struggle to live up to it or so meek they'll lose every job interview at application stage.

OK, it's not easy. But to be honest, there's no point worrying about all of that stuff. Soon enough, the name won't mean anything other than: your child. Because the kid becomes bigger than the name. Arctic Monkeys seemed like a terrible name when they first came out. Then they became the band they are and no one cares. I'm not saying you should call your kid 'Arctic Monkey'.

Just before you commit to the name you like, remember to do the playground test (imagine yelling it across the playground in front of all the other parents and see if you feel embarrassed) and try it with your surname. You'd think that's obvious, but I went to school with a girl called Michaela Taylor. She was asthmatic but refused to carry that little plastic thing around.

And a lot of people like to see what the baby looks like before committing to a final name to make sure the name fits the face. What you don't want to happen is to see your new baby and think, 'Oh damn, we told everyone he was going to be called Oliver, but this baby is definitely an Alan.'

GET YOUR SLEEP IN

In the build-up to the birth, people will be constantly telling you to 'make sure you get your sleep in now' and, while that may seem like the dullest bit of small talk 'humour' since 'you need a holiday to get over the holiday!', it is actually one of the most valuable bits of advice you'll ever receive.

In those last few weeks before the birth, the mum will find it almost impossible to sleep properly. She's in constant physical discomfort and every time she tries to relax, the baby wriggles around. But you don't have this problem. Until the baby turns up, your bedroom is quiet and there's no one relying on you to keep them alive, so sleep. Sleep like you've never slept before. Partly because you're really going to miss these halcyon days when you could close your eyes at 11pm and know that they would stay closed until the sun comes up. But mainly – and less selfishly – because it will really help you both deal with what's to come if at least one of you is well-rested.

OK, well that's everything you need to think about during the main part of the pregnancy. There can be a tendency to try to fill all of your time doing stuff to prepare, because you feel like you should. But once all of the things we have discussed so far are in order, do try to enjoy the times when you've not got much to do. There will be plenty to do soon enough, don't you worry…

CHAPTER 3

HIGH ALERT

The final few weeks of a pregnancy can be a stressful period because you are on high alert at all times and all you want is for your child to get here safely. Even though this period of waiting around can be frustrating, try not to let yourself get too anxious. If there are any problems, the doctors will get involved (remember you can always keep going in to the maternity ward to get checked if you're concerned about anything), so do your best to focus on the nice bits. You'll look back on this time fondly as the last point it was just the two of you. So, try to do some of the things that might be tricky as soon as the baby comes, like sleep (your partner might be too uncomfortable though), romantic walks (your partner might be too uncomfortable though) and the cinema (your partner might be too uncomfortable though). I suppose what I'm saying is, it's a nice time for you. You'll miss having the baby in a contained spot where all of its needs are automatically met, so do your best to relax and enjoy this time as much as you can.

ARE YOU READY FOR THE BIRTH?

Make sure you know the route to the hospital, there is petrol in the car (if you have a car and it takes petrol) and you know how the parking works when you arrive. Ensure you know where the bag is that your partner has packed (she has almost definitely done this before you even thought about it) and you've familiarized yourself with its contents enough that you'll know where to look when your in-labour partner is yelling 'FLANNEL!' After this is all sorted and you know the mum is ready for the birth, it's time to get yourself prepared, both practically speaking and mentally.

JOSH WIDDICOMBE: Like someone cramming for an exam that they know they are unprepared for, I decided to ask my mates what they knew. The week before my wife was about to give birth I sent out a text to all of my dad friends and asked for their top five tips. Very few stick with me (it was a very stressful and tiring time), but there are two tips that I found hugely helpful and try to pass off as my own at any opportunity.

Firstly, when your baby is born, don't put pressure on yourself for it to be this huge Hollywood rush-of-love moment like you have never felt before. I have friends who have felt they have failed as parents from moment one because they haven't felt the magical bond we are all told we will experience. Knowing that if that doesn't happen instantly, it is perfectly natural and doesn't make you a monster is hugely reassuring. You have enough on your plate without worrying about being dead inside.

Secondly, get an insulated cup. Otherwise you will keep leaving your tea to go cold as you change a nappy/clean up some sick/attempt to burp your child.

A bag for you

It's worth also packing yourself a little bag with all the things you'll need for the hospital. Make sure you've got some loose change for the car park and vending machines, a comfy hoody or jacket, a spare T-shirt, a load of snacks, chewing gum, drinks, more snacks and then just a few more snacks.

But maybe don't show your partner, because your 'fun day out' snack bag might wind her up.

GETTING THINGS MOVING

The normal time for a baby to arrive – what they call 'full term' – is between 37 and 42 weeks (around 7 per cent of babies come earlier than this). Pretty vague, I know. It's potentially a five-week window where you're going to have to just wait around for it to come.

You'll probably be sick of the pregnancy by the time it gets to full term and the mum definitely will be, so you might just want things to get moving. Some of the things you'll often hear suggested to help are Indian takeaways and sex. I have no idea if there is any scientific basis to it, and there's no way I'm going to research it and risk disproving it. Neither of them worked for us, but I in no way begrudge the person who suggested them. A friend of mine really pushed his luck and told his wife that he'd heard what can really get things going is a threesome. She agreed to it, so long as he wasn't involved.

There are some techniques to hurry things along that you'll probably be less familiar with, like the one Carl Donnelly experienced:

CARL DONNELLY: Two weeks before the due date, my wife saw that it was a full moon. Being something of a hippy, she told me, 'We should do a full moon ceremony!' I had no idea what that meant, but by midnight we were in the garden surrounded by candles, writing on bits of paper. It was fun, but I assumed that's all it was. We went to bed and early the next morning my wife woke me up saying she was feeling odd. I got up and made some breakfast while checking in regularly on how she was feeling. A couple of hours after getting up, she started to suggest she may be having contractions. I wasn't convinced, but downloaded an app for measuring them just in case. The first time I measured what my wife was feeling, the app informed us she was in labour. We went to hospital and she was 5cm dilated. The long and short of that tale is I think I'm married to a witch.

A sweep

If you are overdue or the medical professionals want you to go into labour early for safety reasons, they sometimes get involved to try to bring on a natural labour. Because my wife developed a condition during pregnancy (something called obstetric cholestasis), they wanted to get the baby out as soon as it was safe to do so. When the time came, they decided to try to get things moving by doing a 'sweep'. I think the term 'sweep' is far too descriptive and not nearly medical enough. It sounds like there were no doctors around to offer a solution, so the caretaker chipped in with an idea. Personally, I prefer medical names to sound mysterious and clever. I'd be a lot less inclined to have an endoscopy if they called it an anal-rodding.

As I'm sure you've guessed, a sweep isn't a very pleasant experience, but I think when a woman gets to this point in the pregnancy, discomfort is all she knows, so she just wants anything that might hurry things along. It involves the doctor or midwife using their finger to sweep around the cervix to try to separate it from the membranes of the amniotic sac that surrounds your baby.

As the dad in this situation, you feel helpless. All you can do is hold her hand and pull a face that says, 'Sorry again'. It's a confusing mix of emotions you feel towards the person doing it. I remember, on the one hand, feeling so grateful to this man for trying to help us that I wanted to hug him, while, on the other, fighting the urge to rugby tackle him to the ground and stuff his stupid glasses up his stupid nose. I did neither. I just hoped it wouldn't last long for my wife and luckily it didn't.

Afterwards he told us he thought that should speed things up a bit. I thanked him and hoped I'd never see his stupid face again.

Induction

If a woman is overdue or she or the baby has a health problem, the doctors might decide to induce her. This involves an oxytocin drip, a pessary (a tablet inserted into her vagina) or pretty much anything else they can think of to get this thing going. It's not easy on the woman because it usually takes absolutely ages. It often means days at home or on the antenatal ward waiting for it to take effect and for labour to start. So, if your partner is being induced, prepare for a long one and pace yourselves.

IS THIS IT?

It's hard to know when it's time to go into hospital. A lot of the signals are unreliable, like false contractions (known as Braxton Hicks), which tell you it's happening, when it's not.

And things like waters breaking, which you expect to

happen, but often don't until later on or not at all and need to be broken by the midwives.

When it was really happening with my wife, it started with a 'pop'. That's how she described it to me. Not painful or anything, just a bit weird. And I think the 'pop' she described was a feeling. I didn't hear anything. But then again, I was watching *The Simpsons* and it was quite loud.

Generally, even when things do get going, you have a lot of time. So, try to stay at home for as long as you can or you risk turning up at the hospital and being told to go home. That's what happened to us. My wife was having contractions every few minutes, so we rushed into hospital. Only to be greeted as if we'd turned up at Glastonbury on a Monday in May. The midwife told us to go home, give it 24 hours and then call them with an update. My wife gave me a look as if to say, 'Is she fucking kidding?' I gave the midwife a look as if to say, 'I don't suppose you're fucking kidding, are you?' She wasn't fucking kidding.

Not only is this extra stress and frustration, but it'll also mean you'll be paying twice for the hospital car park. Now, I know that isn't the most important thing here, but it does leave a sour taste. In fact, while we're on that subject, let's give it a moment because I'm getting annoyed just thinking about it. When I was younger, I assumed that the money you put in the machine was going to the hospital and I could square that with myself. In the same way I feel when I'm asked to sponsor a nephew for his funny face marathon in aid of a donkey sanctuary, it's annoying, but I can come to terms with it because the money is going to those in need. Not so with the hospital car park. It is raising money for millionaire land owners and the people they are targeting are the sick, visitors of the sick and the doctors and nurses who are helping the sick. It's criminal. Anyway, enough about the awful and heartless way our society works and back to the little person you're about to bring into it.

You don't want to be in the position we were in. So, my tip to you would be to stay at home for longer than feels natural. They say that if she can hold a conversation with you, it's still too early to go into hospital. Even if that conversation is just a swear-filled tirade about what a prick you are for getting her into this mess.

You'll know when things are getting serious when your partner starts to make cow sounds. You might have heard them if you've ever watched *One Born Every Minute* or been to Wales. And, in my experience, no midwife takes much notice until a woman starts mooing. My wife used to think that it was bizarre that someone would choose to make that sound and was convinced she wouldn't. But then it comes; there is no choice. A low, bovine moan from deep in the abdomen. Think of this as your air-raid siren. So, if you're in another room and it sounds like your partner has turned the volume up to max on an episode of *Countryfile*, it's time to mobilize. Go, go, go!

CHAPTER 4

THE BIRTH

Before the fifties, it was quite uncommon for fathers to be present at the birth of their kids. They'd sit in the pub, smoking their pipe until they received news of the arrival. Then, they'd visit their wife, give their new baby a firm handshake and have very little to do with it for the next 18 years. For better or worse, that is no longer the way.

It is now very common for the father to be at the birth, and is generally regarded as a good thing for everyone. It provides support for the mum, it is proven to strengthen the bond between father and child, and you'll hear a lot of men say it's the best day of their life. Well, I'm sorry to tell you, a lot of men are either maniacs or liars. Even though the result is probably the best thing to ever happen to you, the process is not one any sane person could find enjoyable.

THE DRIVE

When the moment comes, you'll need to get your partner to the hospital, unless you want to deliver the baby. Pay attention to this bit, because it is very important.

DO NOT FORGET HER HOSPITAL BAG.

Rip out those six words, photocopy them and sellotape them to every door in your home if you need to.

On the way to the hospital you'll feel unprepared. And you are. But that's OK, everyone is. The drive is the thing a lot of dads think about in the build-up to the birth. This is often your responsibility and you probably had visions of speeding through red lights while your partner yells, 'Quick! It's coming!' But, in my experience, you drive much slower and more carefully than usual, as if you've got an unexploded bomb in the passenger seat. And the bomb is looking at you as though it wants to kill you. There were loads of potholes along the route we took, so I was going over them slowly so it didn't jolt my wife too much. But then I suspected she was annoyed that I was going too slowly. So I explained about the issue with the road surface and why I thought it had become such a problem in the area recently and promised that, as soon as this was all over, I'd get in touch with the council about this pothole epidemic and make sure something was done. And she told me to shut the fuck up about the fucking potholes. My tip would be to try to drive as normally as possible and keep any chat about the state of the tarmac to ten minutes, max.

If you don't drive – or even if you do but you're too nervous, tired or drunk – there has never been an easier time to get a taxi if that is a better option for you. Just remember to take the car seat for the way home and, if you can, do it on your partner's account, because there is a chance she will swear a lot, and damage to your Uber rating is permanent.

'HELLO DAD'

Throughout the pregnancy, people would often ask me how I was feeling about it all and I'd reply, 'Yeah, all right actually.' Of course I was all right. Nothing had changed for me. I wasn't the one who was throwing up every morning and having all of my remaining nutrients syphoned off by the bowling ball attached to my front. So, you need to prepare yourself that everything might hit you all at once. For me, it was when we arrived at the hospital and the midwife greeted me by saying, 'Hello *Dad*.' Then another midwife joined in, 'Oh, so this is *Dad*', 'How are you feeling, *DAD*?' I wanted to shout, 'Stop! This is all moving too fast!' It felt like that morning I was young and carefree, then, just a few hours later, I was the dad to two midwives called Janet and Sheila.

On top of this, being called 'Dad' for the first time instantly made me think of all the things I'd wanted to do before I got to this point. How did it happen so quickly? Where did all those years go? The blood drained from my face. My wife (now in labour) offered to get up so I could have a seat. I reluctantly accepted. She asked, 'Are you OK?' I said, 'Yes. I think I'm going to start a band.'

THE WAIT

You've just had the adrenaline rush of getting to the hospital, everything in your head is screaming 'THIS IS IT!', then your partner is examined to see how dilated she is – a word, only ever used for pupils or cervixes, that means it's widening. Now, brace yourself for the number to be much lower than you expect. If it's 1 or 2cm, which, from various anecdotes I've heard, it often is at this point, then there's a long way to go. It means the opening to the cervix is about the size of a blueberry and it needs to get to the size of a bagel. Which reminds me, ration your snacks, it's going to be a while.

The average time for dilation is 0.5–0.7cm per hour, but this is just an estimate and it can be a lot slower or indeed a lot quicker. You'll notice as you go through the process, there don't seem to be any set rules about anything. It's oddly quite comforting that, when you don't know what the hell is going on, neither does anyone else.

My wife's took much less time, which was lucky. But it was so quick, it meant she missed the opportunity to have any proper pain relief, which was unlucky.

PAIN RELIEF

There are several different levels of pain relief on offer during the birth. These are the main ones:

TENS machine

This is a machine you can hire that uses a mild electrical current to give you pain relief. I'm not entirely sure how (and if) it works because we didn't really consider it. They are very popular with mothers who want to stay drug-free, but my wife had something heavier in mind. I was reluctant about this one anyway, because I know that if I hired something, instead of thinking about what I was supposed to be thinking about at the birth (my wife's welfare, the wonder of new life, etc.), I'd have been thinking about return dates and deposits. Not a stress I wanted on top of everything else, thank you.

Water birth

Proponents of water births believe childbirth in water results in a more relaxed, less painful birth. It reduces the pain of labour and the weight the mother feels, and women who have water births are generally less likely to have epidurals. When we did a tour of the hospital my wife was going to give birth in, they told us the dad was welcome to get in the pool too, as long as he wasn't naked. So, if that's what you were planning, get it out of your head right now. You absolute lunatic.

Gas and air

This is everyone's favourite pregnancy drug. Light enough to be used by those wanting a natural birth, but effective enough to instantly make you feel better. You can have as much as you like and it's quite common for dads to have a go on it when the midwife isn't looking. I think that's generally seen as an OK thing to do, just don't hog it.

Pethidine

If gas and air is your gateway drug, this is the hard stuff. A downside is it can make the baby feel a bit drowsy. So, if you do opt for this one, be sure to make sure your newborn doesn't operate any heavy machinery straight away.

Epidural

This is the most extreme. It's an injection to the spine that numbs everything from the waist down, so the mum feels nothing. There is a risk that, because she can't feel anything, she can damage herself by pushing too hard. There's a much smaller risk that the injection won't work and a much, *much* smaller risk that it will work too well and end up permanently numbing things. But this is incredibly rare; some say it's a 1 in 23,000 risk, others say it's closer to 1 in 50,000. This is definitely not one for the dads to have a go on.

LABOUR

Labour hurts, so you're going to have to watch your partner go through a lot of pain. Initially, your instinct will tell you to act – ring an alarm, call the police, thump a midwife; something needs to be done. But it's amazing how quickly you become OK with it. You could be the most caring and empathetic person in the world, but you just can't maintain that level of concern for over ten hours. Eventually, this permanent state of suffering becomes almost normal.*

I guess it's a coping mechanism so you can carry on functioning, but I remember it worrying me just how numb you can become to human pain. It must be how mafia bosses can continue carrying out ruthless hits for decades and Michael Gove can continue doing his job in government.

The average time of labour for a first-time mother is eight to twelve hours. That's more than one full series of *The Sopranos*, with similar levels of tension, nudity, gore and mild peril. But I'm sorry to tell you, not nearly as much Italian food.

ELIS JAMES: Our son was born incredibly quickly – Isy was eating shepherd's pie at 1pm, I went to ask for pain relief at 1.15pm and I was holding him at 1.27pm. Our daughter's birth was more normal, and I don't think I was great. I felt like one of those footballers who is accused of 'going missing in big games'. I repeated the phrases 'Well

---

* I know that's easy for me to say, I wasn't the one with a human slowly making their way through my body.

done', 'Remember to breathe', 'You're doing really well', 'Not long to go now', 'Would you like a drink of water?', 'Remember to breathe', 'That breathing sounds great to me' on a loop for about 12 hours. I'm not exactly sure what a birthing partner should say in those situations, but I'm fairly sure it's not that. It must have sounded like I'd learned English from a book that had lots of pages missing.

MIDWIVES

We had lovely midwives, and the chances are you will too. I think it's the type of career you only get into if you're nice. I don't suppose many are in it for the money or the glamour. Ours were nurturing, supportive, empathetic and experienced enough to not be phased by anything, but still had a sense of appreciation of the magnitude of the whole thing.

Beforehand, I assumed you only had one midwife, but you actually end up having quite a few. Because, at some point during the birth, the midwife who you have bonded with for hours and trusted to be a part of the most intimate, scary event of your entire life, just walks out of the room and doesn't come back. Then a different midwife will enter and pick up where the last one left off, like in a soap where a character goes upstairs then comes back down played by a completely different actor. Your initial reaction is one of betrayal. How could Joanne do this? Did this not mean as much to her as it did to us? Well, no, it didn't. It's her job and she'd finished her shift. She was probably going home to sleep for a bit before coming back and doing this all over again with someone else. It's emotionally taxing enough without staying behind for hours to see every pregnancy through to the end. Anyway, it won't be long before you realize the new one is even better and you instantly forget all about Jenny, or whatever her name was.

The fact that midwives go through the all-consuming experience of birth several times a week for their entire careers is unfathomable to me. I can't imagine the mental strength it would take to deal with the very extremes of human existence every day. They work long, unsociable hours, often without a break. They are constantly responsible for human lives and have to witness some of the most heartbreaking things that can happen in this world, often without the resources they need and certainly without the pay they deserve. Yet they continue to help women through something which feels impossible, and do so while idiots like me stare at them like lost puppies. To all the midwives out there, you are amazing. Thank you.

OTHER TYPES OF BIRTH

Not everyone chooses a natural hospital birth. Some have an elective caesarean, which is where you choose to have a C-section. This relieves a lot of the anxiety about what will happen and when, because what will happen is: a standard procedure that takes around 45 minutes. And when it will happen is: whenever you have booked in for it. This is not to say you won't have all of the other worries, and the recovery is longer. Caesareans aren't quite as safe as natural births either (because it is a major surgery and has all of the associated risks) so a natural birth is usually the recommended route, but C-sections are still very safe.

Home births are increasingly common too. In some countries it's actually the recommended thing to do and, if you want to do it in the UK, it's very easy to arrange with your midwife. Some women find it a lot more comforting to be at home. My wife didn't fancy it and, I have to say, I'm glad. When we left the hospital, she told me she never wants to see that place again. It would've been tricky if she felt that way about our home. And we'd only had our new towels a few months.

WHAT DOES THE DAD DO?

During labour, you will realize that you have very little to offer. And you can tell by the way the midwives are treating you that they would rather you weren't there. I bet it's quite annoying for them. No other department has to put up with this. The heart surgeons don't have some bored dunce wandering about the operating theatre blowing up rubber gloves and asking where the nearest vending machine is.

The midwives are therefore forced to give you made-up jobs to keep you busy. I'm fully aware that the midwife made me Head of Water to make me feel like I wasn't completely surplus to requirements. It's like when the stupid kid at school is given the job of Milk Monitor. (If you were Milk Monitor, I didn't mean that – break time would have fallen apart without you, little buddy!) So, it felt even worse when the responsibility was taken from me.

My dismissal was a result of both 'getting high on my own supply' and messing up the technique. Over the years, I've noticed a lot of people don't tip the bottle enough when giving someone else water from a bottle, which can be very annoying for the recipient. There was no way I was going to make that mistake today because my wife, even though incredibly patient in everyday life, can get a little tetchy when she's giving birth. So, when my moment came, I tipped it right back, gave a firm squeeze, and her eyeballs nearly popped out of her head.

Apart from the water, all you've got in your armoury to help your partner through the birth are a few obvious instructions ('Push!', 'Breathe!'), a damp flannel for patting her hot, angry face and the offer of a massage. But to be honest, giving a massage with the midwives watching feels a little bit embarrassing. I think it's because the only reason I'd usually offer my wife a massage is the hope it would lead to something else, and I was 99 per cent certain that wasn't on the cards.

KERRY GODLIMAN: I think all a dad can do during childbirth is await instructions and know with all his heart that he is redundant. I had a home birth so he had lots to do filling up the birthing pool, which gave him something to focus on. He was so thankful for that sense of purpose.

But no one expects you to do a 'job' as such. All of the important stuff is covered. Yours is a different role. It's purely to make your partner feel like everything is going to be OK and she has the strength to do this. So, you will need to concentrate on playing it cool. The look on your face has to say, 'Everything is totally fine', while the voice in your head yells, 'AAAAAAAARRRRRRRRGGGHHHHHHH. FUUUUUCKKKKK. LET ME OUT! NOW!'

The technique of acting like you know what is going on and everything is all right, so as not to worry the person who is looking to you for reassurance, is one you're going to have to call upon again and again throughout your parenting career. So I hope you're good at it.

But even though it can feel like you're lying when you tell her she can get through it, you're not. No matter how upset she gets, no matter how low her pain threshold in everyday life, she will become an unbreakable warrior when she needs to. Women were built with enormous strength reserves for this exact situation. She can get through it.

MIDWIFE: We don't expect dads to know what they are doing, all we want is for them to support and encourage their partner, and distract her when appropriate. It's nice when they say to staff, 'Tell me if there's anything you want me to do' and it's best if dads stay in the designated chair next to their partner, unless they are asked to do a job or they need to go to the loo (that is allowed).

If you have specific requests then by all means let us know. If you want to see the head crowning, that's fine, we will tell you when it's happening, but from the minute she starts pushing some dads get their head in the way of our vision when it's unlikely they'll see anything for the first half an hour of this bit, so stay up your end!

My ideal dad is a non-smoker, loves his partner, is chatty, excited about being a dad and realizes that this situation is harder on his partner than him. It's also good if he has listened to his partner when she packed the bag and knows roughly where the lip balm and flannels are instead of emptying the suitcase all over like a burglar while she is shouting at him.

Dads should not: talk about their ex-partner's birth (happens a lot) or think they understand hours of contractions because they got banged in the nuts playing Sunday League football. The blokes who say 'we' wanted a water birth or 'we' didn't want an epidural also annoy us.

A lot of dads just sit on their mobile phone which we understand, because it can be boring, but when the woman is in a lot of pain, paying some attention to her and the situation goes a long way.

Some dads totally add to our workload and need more care than the women. Some faint as they were too polite to take their jumper off or don't want to eat and drink in front of us. Please eat and drink! It's not always the man's fault if he adds to the workload, though; I remember having to deal with one occasion where a woman arrived with her partner, then a short while later her husband turned up at the desk.

Shut up and get on with it

This is an extreme experience for you. It'll be an endurance test like you've never had before. You'll be physically pushed, emotionally tortured and extremely sleep-deprived. But the biggest and most difficult test is to never ever mention it. This won't feel natural. You'll want everyone to know it was difficult for you too. Well, don't worry, everyone does know. They just don't really care. Until your vagina starts tearing open, you are still the lucky one, so you're just going to have to deal with it.

When she swears at you, take it. When she insults you, take it. When she says that your new jacket doesn't suit you, you're just going to have to take it, mate. You can sulk, cry and feel self-conscious about your chest-to-arm-size ratio next week, but today you smile supportively and get on with it.

This is your chance to do something amazing. I promise you, it will mean so much to her and she will remember it forever. But if you complain once about being tired, hungry, bored or having an ulcer on your tongue, she will also remember it forever.

It's good to know going in that the whole thing might feel like a life-and-death situation. To me, it seemed like we were constantly on the edge of something terrible. At various points, senior doctors were called in, alarms went off, people filled the room, heartbeats sped up then slowed right down, the baby's head got stuck, levels of oxygen dipped, there was screaming, crying and worry like I've never experienced before. It felt constantly critical. Always a moment away from disaster. Like we were trapped in one long opening scene of *Casualty*. And it turns out that this is all absolutely normal.

In the same way, when you first experience turbulence, you

wonder why everyone isn't screaming and the pilot hasn't made an announcement instructing you all to prepare for your fiery deaths. But then, after a while, you accept that falling miles through the sky in a 400-tonne steel capsule is completely cool and you should just chill out.

I'm not telling you this stuff to scare you. I just want you to know that the things you are programmed to be frightened by in everyday life are par for the course in this situation, so it helps to know what is coming up so you don't freak out too much.

I remember it struck me that the midwives' behaviour was completely at odds with the situation. During what felt like a medical emergency, they were just chatting away and laughing about something else. You'd think that this kind of casual behaviour might be reassuring, but I just worried that they were incredibly bad at their jobs and didn't know what was going on. Or I was being Punk'd. Any moment, Ashton Kutcher would jump out from behind a curtain, my wife would remove her fake pregnant stomach, and we'd all have a bloody good laugh and go home. This, as you can probably guess, didn't happen. It wasn't a trick; they are just so used to this situation, it is normal to them. And *Punk'd* hasn't been on TV for decades.

Rest assured that if there are any serious issues your midwife will talk to you about them. Alarms and urgent calls for doctors are worrying at the time, but be thankful that we live in an age where you can monitor everything that is happening to Mum and baby, and the moment something seems slightly off, the experts will be there to get things back on track. A hundred years ago, you wouldn't have had a specialist nearby. You might have been in a barn with a cow, which will have been less stressful, but definitely more dangerous. To my knowledge, cows are much less able to check that your oxygen levels are normal.

It will appear to you that the mother is going through a trauma from which she'll never recover, but it's exactly what she was designed to do and there's some crazy stuff going on to help her cope. I remember, during the labour, coming to terms with the fact that, even though we'd hoped to have three kids, we would now only ever have one because there was no way my wife would ever go through this again. I had heard a rumour that the female mind blocks out certain parts of the memory of birth as a way of tricking them into doing it again, but assumed it was absolute bullshit. But do you know what; I think it might be true. Within about an hour of the birth, she was already talking about the next one. I wanted to grab her by the shoulders and yell, 'Did you not just see what happened in there?' Biology is amazing. I only wish she could forget other memories as quickly, like the time I got so drunk I passed out and pissed myself, but no, that one seems to be lodged in there for the rest of time.

MIDWIFE: The situation can seem worrying to any birth partner as the rooms are alien to you, but they are our workplace and pretty much all the equipment we use makes sounds. I usually reassure dads by telling them not to worry unless I look worried. That's a bit difficult when we've got face masks on though. Sometimes the room does fill with staff and it can be due to an emergency or just a review with the doctor. But even when it's an 'emergency', most of what we do is pre-empting a problem, so we get the necessary people in before it's an issue. Be reassured we are all there for a safe delivery for Mum and baby.

POSITIONS

When you imagined what the birth would be like, you probably pictured the mother of your baby lying on her back with her legs apart and a sheet covering her for modesty. Well, you need to wake up, son! This isn't the episode of *Friends* where Phoebe gave birth, or the episode of *Friends* where Rachel gave birth, or the time Erica gave birth in that episode of *Friends*; this is real life and she will give birth in whatever position feels right. It might be on her back, but it also might be on all fours, standing up or with one leg on the floor and one in your face. And you will do whatever you can to help. If this means standing there for hours on end acting like a lamp post for her to lean against, then you're just going to have to tense up and do it.

FALSE ALARMS

After a few hours of labour, when my wife had given everything and felt like she couldn't go on much longer, one of the midwives announced she could see the baby's head and my wife should get ready for the final push. The other midwife crouched down like a cricket backstop, ready to catch the baby (because my wife was standing up, not because it fires out, don't worry) and my wife cried with happiness. It had been a long ordeal, but the end was now in sight. She pushed and pushed and then…nothing. So, she carried on pushing, harder than she'd ever pushed before. And we all held our breath. And she pushed. And we held our breath. And she pushed. This went on for over an hour. Then the midwife said she needed to check something. She did an examination and, after a moment, realized that the thing she thought was the head wasn't the head at all. It was the amniotic sac, which meant my wife's waters hadn't even fully broken. My wife burst into tears again. She thought she was seconds away from the end, but we had barely even started. The only consolation was we didn't have a baby with a head that looked like a balloon full of amniotic fluid. School would've been tough for that little fella.

But after this, even though it was the most demoralizing thing that could've happened and my wife felt like she had nothing left, she dug deep and managed to find even more strength. I guess something primal just takes over you and you can deal with anything.

COMPLICATIONS

When unexpected things happen, it can be scary. But every emergency is something these medical staff will have dealt with hundreds of times and they know the route out of it.

You'll worry about the danger your partner and your baby are in, but the maternal mortality rates show fewer than 10 in every 100,000 women dies during pregnancy and childbirth in the UK, with heart disease being the leading cause, so it's incredibly rare that something just goes wrong on the day. With babies, the rates show that in the UK there are 4 stillbirths in 1,000 and this is getting lower all the time. Despite the stats though, it will still be scary when there are complications.

Sometimes women will go in with a pre-existing condition which means they need to be monitored more closely, sometimes there's a planned C-section and sometimes there's a development during the process which means the safest thing to do is to have an emergency C-section.

Sometimes the baby doesn't play ball, they are tired, their heart rate drops or they are in a weird position – transverse (sideways) or breech (bottom or feet first) – so the delivery plan might have to change. If the baby just needs a bit of help, they might decide to do a forceps or ventouse delivery (where they attach a vacuum cup to the baby's head). They then pull the baby out with the help of the mum's pushing. In the case of deliveries like this, it's fairly common that an episiotomy is needed. This is when they have to cut the vaginal opening to make it bigger. I'll end this section here because you are probably wincing so hard you can no longer see.

MIDWIFE: If a woman goes to theatre and we need to do an emergency caesarean there are categories of urgency depending on the situation. If we want to get the baby out quickly and there is no time for a spinal (epidural) the woman has a general anaesthetic (she's put to sleep) and the partner is not allowed in theatre, mainly because seeing a loved one having a breathing tube inserted is not pleasant, even though the woman is sedated so knows nothing about it. It means Dad is left in a room on his own, so it can be worrying for him. Usually another member of staff on the ward will make sure he's OK, but they are to be reassured that the staff need to be with the partner to get a safe delivery of the baby. Once the baby is out, a staff member will come and tell Dad that all is well. If things are not OK, he will be kept up to date throughout, but dads can always ask questions whenever they like.

It's horrible, but sometimes babies do die. If the worst should happen, parents are told straight away and counselled at every point through the journey. But we do absolutely everything to make sure this happens as rarely as possible and, thankfully, there has been no safer time in human history to give birth.

WANT TO WATCH?

A lot of people will urge you to watch the moment of birth and tell you it's the most beautiful, magical, unforgettable moment you'll ever witness. I was happy to take the risk that it wasn't and wait the extra ten seconds so that the first time I saw my baby it was *without* a vagina around its head. So, I can't tell you what it's like. But I can imagine it and it's really weird. When I discussed it with my wife before the birth, she said she'd prefer me not to watch that bit and I replied, 'I'm happy with whatever makes you feel most comfortable' while, in my mind, I was doing Stuart Pearce's penalty celebration from Euro '96.

IT'S HERE!

Your baby finally arriving is a moment you will never forget. Your partner has achieved something that at times looked impossible and it's hard to describe just how in awe of her you'll be in this moment. The feeling of pure relief is overwhelming. But all of this emotion can sometimes cause dads to behave stupidly.

ADAM KAY: I think the gold medal goes to a dad who, on watching baby crowning, shouted, 'Where's its face?!', causing the mum to scream, the baby to fly out uncontrolled and a rather big tear to occur. Turns out the baby's face was fine and was located – as is traditional – on the front of its head. (Babies are generally born facing down, by the way.) Seen and not heard, thanks, dads.

The feeling of relief can be short-lived for some people, who are about to experience a new, even bigger worry. If you don't hear the baby cry straight away, like you assume is normal, it can be heart-stopping. It's the thing you are waiting for to let you know the baby is alive and well. It's what needs to happen to kick-start their lungs. So, when they don't (combined with them looking blue), it makes for a worrying few seconds, let me tell you.

This was the first moment I realized just how much this little thing instantly meant to me. I would have died right there and then to make my baby live. Even now, I feel sick at the memory. It is quite possibly the worst single moment I've ever had. But that's because I didn't know beforehand that I should have half-expected this to happen.

The truth is, sometimes the baby cries straight away and sometimes it can take a few seconds or even minutes. The poor baby doesn't know how it's meant to act. It hasn't seen all of the rom coms you've seen. It didn't exist in the real world until a few moments ago and, already, you're putting it under pressure to act like the fake perfect Hollywood births. Jesus, give the kid a break.

Our midwives didn't seem phased though and, within a few seconds (months, in my memory), our baby started crying. Then we started crying. And it was the best moment of my life.

We asked the midwife if it was a boy or girl and she told us to take a look. But all we could see was the bum. The midwife was amused by this and said, 'What do you think it is?' My wife, who, it's fair to say, wasn't really in the mood for playing a guessing game at this point cried, 'Please just tell us.' The midwife said, 'It's a boy!' and we were both delighted. Obviously, I would have been very happy with a girl, but, you know.

Then we got to have a proper look at our child for the first time. Battered, bruised and with a head squished into a long cone shape. I didn't know whether to be upset, amused or suspicious my wife had had an affair with Bert from *Sesame Street*.

Try not to judge your baby for the way it looks in this situation. They have been through a lot. Remember how fucked up Andy Dufresne looked when he finally got out of that pipe in *The Shawshank Redemption*? Now imagine how he'd look if that pipe was narrower than the circumference of his own head.

This squashed, swollen alien, who will probably be lathered in a white sort of paste (something called vernix) and might even be covered in fine, soft hair (why does no one mention this?!), is both the weirdest and most beautiful thing you've ever seen. Thankfully, the unique beauty that baby has when it's first born isn't permanent and it will go on to have a much more conventional human look in the coming days and weeks.

Cutting the cord

Over the years, it has become 'the done thing' for the father to cut the cord. I imagine this is a charitable attempt from healthcare professionals to rebuild the fragile ego of the sensitive bloke who feels like he has offered nothing. Now everyone will play along and pretend they really need your big strong grip for this last bit. They just wouldn't be able to manage it with their weak little hands.

It is a job that makes you feel very important, like opening a stiff jar or reaching up to a high shelf but, in truth, a chimp could do it. The midwife will give you the option and they really don't care if you do it or not. But if you want to, they will make it very simple for you. All you have to do is cut. It's worth bearing in mind the cord is probably a bit tougher than you'd imagine, kind of like cutting a large electrical wire. There you go, I've made it feel even manlier for you. You can't really mess it up, but for a smooth cut, just do it confidently and firmly, and don't, whatever you do, say, 'I now declare this vagina officially reopened.'

INITIAL CHECKS

The midwives do a test on the baby one minute after they are born and again five minutes after they are born, called the Apgar Score, and this is a quick, simple way of assessing the health of a newborn. They check the heart rate, muscle tone and any other signs to see if any medical or emergency care is needed.

You'll also be offered a vitamin K injection for your baby straight after the birth to prevent a rare blood disorder in newborns. It's incredibly safe, but if you don't want your baby to have an injection for any reason, they can give vitamin K orally in several doses over the following few weeks.

Premature babies and special care

Sometimes babies are born way ahead of schedule and sometimes they have a health issue or disability at birth, which means they need to go to the special care baby unit (SCBU), the local neonatal unit (LNU) or the neonatal intensive care unit (NICU), depending on the level of care they need. Here, they will be constantly looked after until they are ready to go home with you.

There's no doubt you will be sick with worry if your baby goes into a special care unit and you will stay that way for the entire time they are there. But it really is so wonderful that there is a place purpose-built to do everything to help your baby and provide them with everything they need to build up their strength and health as quickly as possible.

THE PLACENTA

I'm afraid the cord-cutting ceremony doesn't quite mark the end of labour. There is still the placenta to deal with. The woman will essentially have to give birth again to get this out. This is another thing they don't feature in sitcoms. Although, having gone through it, I can see why. It's not really something that would work with a laughter soundtrack on it.

All being well, this will be a lot easier than the birth and, even though it's a fair old thing to push out, many women report hardly noticing it. Contractions usually continue (to push the placenta forward), but they shouldn't be as big as the earlier ones. And, in most cases, it will be out within five minutes. Some people keep the placenta, some plant it in the ground and some even eat it. These people should be avoided at all costs.

There is a small chance the placenta won't come away from the uterus, though. This was the case with my wife. And there seem to be a few different ways of getting it sorted. The first one was like something I do if there's a problem round the house, with a radiator or whatever: just wait and see if it sorts itself out. And it often does. (The placenta, not the radiator. The radiator is fucked.) If it still doesn't come, they can give the mother an injection in her thigh with something to speed up the process, and this is usually very effective. If this doesn't work, they do it again.

But if this doesn't work, the final thing to do, which is what we ended up having to do, is go into theatre for a manual removal. When they first mention this, it can seem terrifying. You thought the danger was over, but the word 'theatre' conjures up images of scalpels, blood and surgeons with a single bead of sweat dropping down their heads, shouting 'Stat! We're gonna lose her!' Or, worse, drama students telling you about their feelings. But this is neither.

They invited me and our new baby in to watch. Well, maybe not watch, but to chat to my wife and comfort her and keep her mind off the fact that several people were about to reach into her abdomen through her vagina.

The theatre isn't nearly as scary as you'd imagine. It's a bright, large, clean place and it seems like loads of happy pleasant people are milling around. It instantly made me feel more relaxed and I could tell it took away a bit of the anxiety for my wife. She had to have a spinal drip for this bit (basically, an epidural). After managing to get through the entire birth on just gas and air, I think it'd be an understatement to say that she found this irritating.

As they were setting up and the friendly anaesthetists were chatting to my wife, I helped (ha!) with the first checks they do on the baby. This is the newborn and infant physical examination (NIPE), which is usually carried out within 72 hours of the birth in hospital, then again at 6–8 weeks with your GP. It was stuff like measuring his arms, counting his testicles (mine had two, which, in this department, I've always considered to be the magic number) and just generally checking he has all the things a baby human is supposed to have. They also do a newborn hearing test, which is done by putting an earpiece on your baby and playing some clicking sounds.

Then, they performed the procedure to get the placenta out. There was nothing glamorous about it. It was a shitload of pulling and yanking. All the feelings from the birth started once more. The urge to want to protect my wife, even though the people who were doing this to her were helping her. And the trick I'd recently learned of smiling to my wife even though, out of the corner of my eye, I could see the live version of *Alien*.

But soon enough, it was out. My wife was safe, my baby was safe and we were in the recovery room eating toast and drinking tea. The tea was too milky, full of sugar and the best thing we had ever tasted.

Once the placenta is out, there's a chance your partner may need stitches if there was a tear or episiotomy during the birth, which takes even more time and involves even more gore.

ELIS JAMES: When my daughter was seconds old, the doctor said, 'Get a vest on this baby, it's cold in here.' The midwife beamed and said, 'Why don't we ask Dad to do it!' I had held very young babies before, but never ones whose age you measured in minutes. I held her like she was the Turin Shroud, and couldn't get the vest over her head because I was terrified her neck would just come off in my hands. After a few minutes of struggling, the midwife said, 'Oh come here, let me do it,' and I remember thinking, 'Oh God...if I can't even *put a vest* on her, we're in trouble here.'

GET YOUR TOP OFF, MATE

Like Ryan Giggs after his goal against Arsenal in the 1999 FA Cup semi-final, the first thing you should do to celebrate the birth of your child is take your top off. But instead of swinging it around your head and running around the ward, fold it up neatly, put it on a chair and cuddle your new child. This skin-on-skin contact is great for bonding and provides enormous comfort to your new baby.

It will make them feel safe and warm, it reduces crying, helps regulate the baby's temperature and heartbeat, and stabilizes blood sugar levels. All by biological magic, without you doing a thing. It's the perfect bit of dadding. Skin-on-skin cuddling has benefits for you too. It releases chemicals to make you happy and bond with your baby. It decreases stress and even the risk of depression.

The midwives really encourage the topless bonding, so it must be good. Or they just fancy a laugh. Either way, it feels very caveman-like, so I recommend it. It might just be worth doing a couple of jogs during the pregnancy so your baby doesn't embarrass you by trying to latch on to your man boob. I joke, but it is quite likely this will happen at some point and it is no reflection on how far you might have let yourself go over the last few months. It's just a reflection of the fact that you have a nipple.

So, there you have it. This is the point you have probably been thinking about for years – you are now a dad. It will feel like you have just been through the weirdest experience of your life, but from now on, the weird new experiences just keep on coming.

CHAPTER 5

THE FIRST WEEK

So, now you've got a baby. You might look at it in your arms and instantly feel a connection and love or you might not. How you deal with the initial feelings of becoming a dad will be unique to you, but you'll likely have tonnes of different emotions flying all over the place. Maybe you'll just want to stare at your baby forever, maybe you'll feel too nervous to hold it or maybe you'll feel more detached than you expected. Maybe you'll start crying and not really know why. That's fine. It's all fine. All of the emotions will settle down soon.

LETTING EVERYONE KNOW

Once you have your baby in your arms and your partner is recovering, you'll probably look at your phone and see that you have a lot of texts and missed calls from friends and family desperate to know that the baby has arrived safely. It's your job to deliver the news. Sending a picture of your new little person is a nice thing to do, but for some reason, a lot of people seem obsessed with knowing the weight. Maybe it's because it's a rough indicator of how healthy the baby is and how the birth might have gone. It's often women who ask about the weight and I think a lot of them actually quite like hearing the horror stories of labour, so maybe in a sense they are asking, 'Just how much did that vagina go through?'

WHAT A BABY LOOKS LIKE

I've already mentioned how battered and bruised your baby looks (which will settle over the first week or so) and the white vernix they might be covered in (as tempting as it will be, don't try to wash this off). But there's also the general appearance of a baby. We've all heard that phrase, 'a face only a mother could love' and I hope your kid hasn't got one of those, but if they have, you won't know because, no matter what, your baby will be beautiful to you.

I remember seeing a picture of a friend's baby. I assumed he'd used some kind of app to make it have an old man's head. A bit of a weird thing to do to a newborn baby, I thought, but it was funny. Then I met the baby in real life and either technology has advanced so far that you can apply the filter in real life or his kid actually did look like Joe Pesci. The parents had no idea.

We drove away, with me saying to my wife, 'Surely they *must* know though, right?' Then I arrived home and looked at a picture of my baby from when he was a few months old and, I have to say: a lot more Gollum-like than I remember. At the time I thought he was the most beautiful thing in the world and I'd walk the streets expecting to be stopped by baby model scouts. I bet all our friends were driving home saying, 'They *must* know, right?'

Luckily, he's beautiful now. Or at least, I think he is. But what a nice quirk of biology. It means even the weirdest-looking things get to feel gorgeous.

ONE LAST NIGHT TO YOURSELF

Women stay in hospital with their baby for a day or so after the birth, on average. But if the birth has been really straightforward, it can be as little as a few hours. If the baby needs to be monitored or Mum needs a bit more recovery time, say if she's had a C-section, it can be a few days.

If Mum and baby have to stay in hospital, you probably won't be allowed to stay there with them. That means she will likely be terrified to be left alone with a newborn while you get the night off, so be as reassuring and supportive as you can.

It also means you'll have at least one last night alone. And what a weird night it is. When you return home on your own, everything is the same as when you left it, but everything has changed.

I've never been so tired as the first night after the birth. Where my wife had the forces of nature working to make sure she remained alert to keep her baby alive, I was just really, really sleepy and had to pull the car over minutes from home to have a nap. When I finally got back, a hunger that had been building for 30 hours took over. I made a pasta meal that I used to eat all the time when I lived alone, but stopped when I moved in with my wife. I'd been dreaming of it for hours and it's only when I write about it now that I wonder if it wasn't one last freak-out about saying goodbye to my old life. It was the most delicious thing I'd ever seen, covered in creamy tomato and mascarpone sauce with a huge pile of grated cheese on top. The first mouthful was heaven. But that was all I had because, for the only time in my life, I fell asleep eating a plate of food. I woke up an hour or so later and the cold food was on the floor in front of my slumped body. I still grieve for that pasta.

CARL DONNELLY: My wife and daughter were kept in overnight which meant, sadly, I was given my marching orders. I got a taxi home where the poor driver had to hear me talking non-stop about what had just happened (the adrenaline of witnessing a birth takes two days to wear off, I found). When I got home and unpacked the bag, I realized I had the placenta in a piece of Tupperware. We didn't have actual plans for it, but thought it would be fun to take it home and find something interesting it could be used for. I went to put it in the freezer, only to find it was full as we'd stocked up loads, prepped for those early months of parenthood. In the bottom freezer drawer there was a bag full of vegetable scraps (for making stock) which I thought was the best thing to make way. That's how I found myself at midnight, on the night of my daughter's birth, celebrating by making a massive batch of vegetable stock. It wasn't the champagne and cigar affair I'd imagined in my youth.

LEAVING HOSPITAL WITH YOUR BABY

When you're waiting to go home from hospital with your baby, you'll have a strange contradictory set of feelings. You are desperate to get out, but you feel institutionalized and you're terrified you're not ready. In hospital you've got the safety of medical staff wandering round doing regular checks, a little alarm you can ring whenever you like and the baby is in a nice, safe, see-through plastic cot that looks reassuringly like a gerbil tank.

But eventually a midwife will wander in and say, 'OK, you can go home,' and you will think 'Thank God' and 'Oh fuck' at the same time. But if you're feeling like you don't know if you can do it, it might be quite reassuring to look around the hospital at all of the other families. Pick the ones who look the least like parents and think to yourself, 'Well, if they can…'

I've found that this is actually a good way to approach all situations when you're worried about doing something new. You don't need to know you're going to be the best at it; you just need to see some people who are definitely going to be worse than you.

The walk out of the hospital is an unusual experience. The first thing that surprises you is just how heavy and awkward it is to carry a baby in a car seat. I'm sure I've seen shots on Instagram of Dwayne 'The Rock' Johnson carrying one heroically from the hospital (his own, I presume) and it looks like a piece of piss. Now, admittedly, I don't have the same physique as The Rock, but it felt like I almost couldn't manage it. It weighs a tonne and the handle is about two feet away from your body, so your centre of gravity is all off. You will naturally want to sling it over your shoulder, but you can't really, so you just have to tense up and hold your breath as you shuffle along the corridor, feeling your spine slowly bend to the left. Don't worry, though, you'll only have to do this on a million more occasions with the weight getting slightly heavier each time.

As you struggle with this, your poor partner will be left to uncomfortably waddle out to the car park, carrying everything else. Somehow, she will have managed to accumulate stuff while bed-bound and she'll be loaded up like Buckaroo with bags of washing, presents and a balloon that feels sarcastic, because she feels like crying as she looks at you trying and failing to get the car seat in the car because you didn't practise it (see Chapter 1!)

Once you're finally in the car and you've paid for that (fucking) car park you need to drive home. You're in a dream-like state and carrying the most precious cargo you've ever had. Prepare for the most careful drive of your life where you'll be scared of everything and will drive so slowly that you can get halfway up a speed bump, then roll back down.

THE FIRST FEW DAYS AT HOME

Initially, you are in the trenches and just go into survival mode. If you were well prepared enough, you'll have some batch-cooked meals in the freezer. If not, phone a friend or family member to bring you some food, or just order in. You need to take the responsibility to make sure your partner is eating well (or at least eating) because she'll be focused on making sure the baby is.

At the very start, your partner might struggle to sleep even when the baby is because she's worried something will happen. Then you might feel too guilty to sleep because you know you'll be leaving her awake fretting, so then neither of you sleep. If this happens, within a short amount of time, emotions will be all over the place and everything will feel much more difficult. I promise you that after a bit of sleep, everything is just so much more manageable.

If you do nothing else, you must sleep and eat. Sometimes doing these things will feel selfish, but you can't pour from an empty cup. You need to stay physically well enough to function and support your new family. So, discuss it with your partner and work out a way you can both try to get some sleep.

Expect anything that isn't essential – like showering or getting changed – to go out of the window in the first few days (and weeks). They are activities for people with no responsibilities. I look back on photos of that time and I look like Tom Hanks in *Cast Away*, but without his sanity.

SINDHU VEE: Take care of your partner over and above every other thing in this universe. Watch her and be available. Be ready to do what she needs when she asks (not when you think she should need it). Be ready to hear that you are not doing things right and then right them. Be ready to agree that you are never *more* tired than your partner, even if she has had a 40-minute nap while you tried to calm a wailing, puking baby. Be ready to put your partner first and yourself third (if you have twins, fourth; triplets, fifth, and so on).

And understand that when you take care of your partner in this way, you are not ministering to someone who 'can't manage on her own' or 'needs you from a place of exhausted weakness'. No. It's not so much about your partner's capabilities – teen mothers in war-torn hellholes manage to produce babies and care for them away from enemy eyes – it's about you PROVIDING AND PROTECTING the most robust, healthy and safe environment for your new baby to experience 'the world' through. You know all those thoughts you had growing up and which society also drilled into you – that fathers provide and fathers protect...well, it's absolutely true: you provide an environment where the mother of your child comes first. Yes, ahead of the seed of your loins, because, if mama breaks, the baby breaks and so do you. Postnatal depression is as much about environment as it is about anything 'organically' to do with the mother herself.

Women and men are equal and must share parenting equally blah blah blah is all true and fine, but do not for a moment think that you are equal as parents to a newborn. You are not. The hard (and it is very hard to accept as a new, excited, devoted father) truth is that your baby 200 per cent wants its mother more than s/he wants you. Full stop. Don't try to compete with your partner for that attention. It will hurt all of you. Instead, try to make sure this ravenous hunger for its mother that an infant has can be experienced as comfortably as possible (and sometimes it's hellish) by your partner. Make the creation of that space your focus; not 'But I'm a parent too! What about me?' Understand that a child's connection and need for each parent changes as they grow. Your time to be centre stage, the parent that is the most needed, the one who is most 'wanted', will come, and, luckily for you, most likely it won't be accompanied by shitting, puking and wailing all night (unless your teen is having a very bad trip, in which case it's even more gross than when they were a baby and please have a stern word with them in the morning, plus call their friends' parents – you adults need to talk).

No matter how much your partner wanted to have this baby, no matter how 'good at it' she is, no matter how easily milk is gushing out of her boobs, no matter how much love is shining out of her when the baby gurgles, no matter how deeply you think she is sleeping (she is not sleeping deeply, she just looks like that because her body is exhausted to the point where, if it wasn't for an infant she just produced, she would be in a medical coma), the fact is every fibre of her being is overwhelmed (some of it even away from her own awareness) by the entire process of having produced another person. At a cellular level. *THIS is the environment you have to make yourself an asset in.* So, set your needs/ wants/hopes aside for the moment (without resentment, please – their time will come), make your partner laugh (often and hard is best), take her irritation (wrath) much, much less personally than you would like to, find a way to make sure your mother/aunt/sister is a salve under the circumstances (ditto her family – step up here without fear because she will thank you later) and be ready to eat and sleep and wake when it suits your partner.

You have to be the hero she needs so she can be the hero your child will demand she be.

BREAST, BOTTLE OR BOTH?

There are some very strong views on breast versus bottle. But you've just got to do the thing that will make everything as manageable as possible for the mum and will get the baby fed. If she can breastfeed, that's brilliant. It's been doing a solid job since the start of the human race, so you can be pretty sure it's good stuff and it's got exactly what the baby needs. It's also healthy for the mum and great for bonding. It can be difficult, though, and there are lactation consultants and midwives who should be able to help.

But if she can't breastfeed – and there are a lot of reasons why it might be difficult – or she doesn't want to, your partner shouldn't beat herself up about it and you shouldn't make her feel bad. Formula is still a good choice. It's better and closer to the real thing than it has ever been and it means Mum is less restricted, you can do a lot of the feeds yourself and it has the benefit of letting you know exactly how much the baby has had.

You don't have to just pick one, though. It's very common for parents to combine them both – known as 'mixed feeding' – which is another brilliant option.

My wife was determined to try to breastfeed and she did, but it wasn't easy. It felt like there was pressure from the medical professionals and society in general, but not always a lot of support. So, in the early days, there were some frustrating moments. Babies can have trouble latching on and the breasts can produce milk at different rates, making it distressing for Mum and baby.

When the baby doesn't take the milk, the mum can feel like she is failing, even though it's nothing to do with what she's doing. There can also be medical issues that develop, like mastitis (when the breast becomes swollen, hot and painful), which make it even more difficult and can make the mum ill. So, your job is just to encourage her, offer help and support her through what is a very big challenge.

Heads up – formula smells awful. It's kind of like off milk, which can give you the impression it *is* off milk. I had no idea about this and was convinced we'd bought a dodgy batch, so we got some more. Another dodgy batch! What are the chances? Then a friend told us that's just how it smells and I was sent to root it out of the bin. I think I was expecting something more like Nesquik.

When do you stop breastfeeding?

This is mainly up to the woman doing it. She might have a plan from the start – for example, she'll agree to do six months, but any longer would restrict her life too much and stop her from finally having that drink, which she definitely deserves. Or maybe she will just carry on until it feels like the right time. There's no set age to stop, but when you feel scratching from their stubble, it gets a bit weird. When you stop, you can move on to formula or wean on to solids, depending on their age.

WIND

Your baby will have wind problems at one time or another, so you will need to help them to burp. If you're anything like me, you'll be inclined to skip any job that doesn't feel essential and it can be very easy to convince yourself that stopping feeds for a burp isn't essential, especially at night. But it will cost you in the long run, when your baby is in a bad mood or in pain all night and you feel guilty because it's your fault. So, you'll need to rub and pat their back to work those burps out early on and save both of you problems later. You'll figure out the best technique for your baby. For one of ours, it was sitting him on my lap with one hand on his chest while I gave him firm pats on the back, starting at the bottom and moving up, as if chasing the burp out. For the other, it was simply sitting her upright, with her back to my stomach, and waiting.

There's always a danger of puke (officially called 'posseting'), especially in the first few months. Some babies are more pukey than others. But it's always best to have a muslin with you when feeding and you should definitely put one on you when burping. Otherwise, you might spend the day walking around looking like a giant seagull has shat all over your back.

You have to help babies fart too because, as you've probably realized by now, they are unbelievably lazy. There are loads of videos on the internet about how you can help them using baby massage, which involves gently rubbing their tummy as well as stretching and moving their legs around. It's easy to do, it relieves the wind and it's great for bonding. But it will also make you feel quite jealous of babies. Imagine being massaged by giant hands that are almost as big as your entire upper body. Lucky little bastards.

Again, you'll find the techniques that work best for your baby. For mine, it was lying them on their backs and tucking their legs towards their chest, then stretching them out in the air. I liked to think of it like I was a physio helping a key player before the second half of extra time in a World Cup knockout match, but maybe you won't need to imagine you are doing something football-related to add interest. Maybe nurturing your baby is enough for you.

HOW YOU CAN HELP

If you have a partner who is breastfeeding, it's hard to know how to assist with the feeds. As much as you want to and you're prepared to put in the effort, it's highly unlikely you'll be able to manage lactating. So, instead you'll have to look for other ways to support your partner. One of the benefits of bottle-feeding is that dads can do their fair share of the feeds and, if the mum is doing them, you can make up the bottles and wash/sterilize them.

If your partner is exclusively breastfeeding, you could offer to do any changes or winding that need to be done either side of the feeds. I also took on the role of logging all of the feeds. This isn't essential, but we were worried our baby wasn't feeding enough and wasn't doing it equally on each breast, so decided to monitor it for a bit. You can get apps that do this simply and easily, but I decided I'd feel better about the work I was doing if I gave it an army vibe.

And so, I always had a little khaki notebook with me, full of lines and lines of my detailed log. It would be things like 'LEFT: 14:12–14:28 16 mins' over and over again. The use of the 24-hour clock made me feel like I was in 'Nam even though I was wearing sweatpants and my wife's fluffy dressing gown. I would do this through the night then look back on the notes and sometimes they'd make no sense. In my half asleep state I'd either write some kind of gibberish like 'LEFTLZ 248?' or stuff from my subconscious would filter through and I'd have notes like 'RIGHT: 02:18 – buy a camper van'.

While we're on the subject of night feeds and sleep, I should tell you about the 'Moro reflex', which is likely to wake your baby at points too. This is a normal thing (but can look quite unusual) and is when a baby suddenly jolts their arms and/or legs out like they are startled. There is no way to prevent it and it's a healthy sign because it shows their nervous system is developing. But you can help soothe them in the night and stop this from waking them by swaddling them – wrapping them snugly in a blanket or muslin with their arms by their side to make them feel safe and secure like they were in the womb.

CHANGING A NAPPY

Here's the stuff you'll need: a nappy, a nappy bag, baby wipes (or wet cotton wool), barrier cream, a changing mat and a baby.

Open the new nappy up ready, lie the baby on their back, undo the tabs on the front of the nappy they are wearing, then hold their ankles (with one hand) and gently lift their bum off the mat (they are really light, so this is quite easy). Survey the atrocity, then wipe them with baby wipes until they are clean, roll up the dirty nappy into a sort of disgusting burrito and put it in the bag. Make sure that all of the baby's creases are clean and, if your baby has a rash, apply some cream. Then slide the new nappy under your baby and fasten the tabs around the front. The tabs can be refastened on most nappies, so if it's crooked you can just redo it to straighten it up. Dress your baby again, then walk to the outside bin with a 'this is gross' look on your face, chuck it in (the nappy bag, not the baby) and forget that it ever happened. Unless, of course, your partner wasn't around. In that case you're probably going to want to bring up just how awful it was for you several times throughout the day.

It's also worth mentioning the difference between boys and girls. Like a lot of dads, I initially felt more comfortable changing my son's nappy than my daughter's because, as I said to my wife much too loudly one time when we were out in public, I know what I'm doing with a penis. But if you've got a daughter, you'll soon get used to changing her nappy too. Make sure that, with a girl, you always wipe from front to back to avoid any risk of infection.

Before you become a dad, changing nappies is a job you don't want to do because you think it'll be disgusting. And yes, it is. But you will actually start to prefer tasks like this because of their clear start and end points. So many dad jobs are vague, meandering and never-ending, so you'll be glad of something with such a clearly defined purpose: clean the shit off the bum. When it's finished, you can take a step back and admire a job well done. Don't do it for too long though or your baby will get self-conscious and passers-by will get concerned.

I'm not saying there aren't hazards and unexpected complications from time to time, though. For some reason, boys especially are triggered when the cooler air hits them and they instantly start to piss. Girls sometimes do it too, but because of the differences between male and female anatomy (I won't go into that now because hopefully you know), when a lad has a piss it will jet out towards wherever the little hose is pointing. You'll notice I used the phrase 'little hose' there. This brings us on to another subject…

What do you call your baby's private parts?

There is an NHS Trust video on this very subject that encourages parents to refer to them by their correct, medical names. They say it's too confusing for kids if we use another 'child-friendly' name. Maybe so, but if I hear a bloke refer to his baby daughter's 'vulva', I'm going to give that bloke a wide berth.

Maybe someday we'll get there, but right now it feels like using the correct term is way too weird for most people, so you end up having to use a cute/silly name instead. It seems a lot simpler to do this for boys. 'Willy' and 'winky' are the most universally accepted names. They are childlike, but not embarrassing to say. Perfect. But I don't think there is a standard for a girl. A lot of the words seem too grown-up; some of them have been sexualized in a way 'willy' and 'winky' haven't. Some are used as insults, and some just seem ridiculous. A list of suggestions from an online forum in response to an anonymous user (not me) with the exact same problem (OK, it was me) are as follows: foof, floof, little bum, front bum, wee wee, Penelope, twinkly, minky, pompey, tuppence, flower, fairy. There is no way a dad could suggest any of these and it not seem very weird. So, best to defer this one to the mum if you can and just pray that she doesn't choose 'Penelope'.

We ended up with 'minky', mainly because we had our daughter second and it rhymed with 'winky'. It's still a bit embarrassing to say, but I've realized that it's incredibly rare that you need to say it in front of anyone other than your family, so as long as you have all decided on the word together and won't laugh at each other, then it's fine.

Meconium

Babies drink their own pee while they are in the womb. That's what most of the fluid is surrounding them, mixed in with a bit of skin, hair and other stuff. They drink it, pee it out, then drink it again. Yes, your baby is gross, mate.

It means the first crap they have when they are out in the real world is some stuff called meconium and it will (hopefully) be the strangest crap you have ever had to clear up. It can be quite a shock when you first see it and you might suspect the baby has been at your secret stash of Marmite and Guinness. It's greenish-black and so thick it doesn't actually feel like you are cleaning up shit at all, more like when you see people on the news washing oil and tar off baby birds on a beach somewhere. And it's often odourless, so it's not actually as bad as you might think. Just have a lot of wipes ready.

Nappy rash

A baby's bum is squishy and soft and funny to look at. Like Donald Trump. But it is also overly sensitive and full of shit. Like Donald Trump. And it doesn't take long for it to get all red and angry-looking. I won't say it again.

If you leave a dirty nappy unchanged for too long – if they've gone in the night, for instance – it can lead to them getting a very, very sore arse. It's surprising how quickly the skin can get a rash and even break. So, if you think your baby (or anyone you love) has had a crap in the night, you need to see to it immediately even though it will be difficult and you'll want more than anything to ignore it. Waking a sleeping baby and changing a dirty nappy are the very last things you'll feel like doing when you've got your warm, comfy bed in your sights. But I promise it's so much better in the long run to do it now. Nappy rash can last for days and days. By nipping it in the bud (or butt), you can save your child a lot of discomfort and you can ensure you don't spend the next week up every night with a crying baby and your own guilt because the reason their bum is causing them so much pain is because you left them.

Shit

Babies are disgusting. They have no manners. They let all of their bodily functions happen without embarrassment. But there is something liberating about spending all your time with a person who is so untethered by society's stuffy rules. Someone who will happily cough in your mouth, piss in your face and shit *everywhere*. It's *so* disgusting and inappropriate, you can't help but laugh at the madness of it all.

You will have to deal with a lot of your baby's shit. But it's not that bad for the first few months when all they are having is milk. It's not really like proper crap at all, there isn't much of it and it's not particularly bad-smelling, although it can be explosive and I don't know any parent who hasn't had to deal with one that has gone all the way up their baby's back, to their neck and then, inevitably, all over their dad. It's gross, but a nice excuse to have a rare shower.

There's no denying it gets worse later on when they start to eat proper food, but by this point, you will have become quite attached to them so you'll forgive them. It's another of those aspects of parenting that eases you in slowly, until one day you're sitting on the floor covered in someone else's shit, thinking to yourself, 'Well, how did we get here then?'

PREPARE FOR THE UNEXPECTED

I'm not sure if people usually get told this, but I didn't have a clue: newborn babies can be affected by the mum's hormones for the first few weeks. It's not uncommon for a baby's breast area to swell and for fluid to leak from them (something they call witch's milk) and their genitals can also swell and get puffy. Newborn girls can also have other temporary effects to the vagina area. It can produce a white fluid and there could even be a bit of bleeding. All of this is absolutely normal, but all of it is absolutely horrifying if you haven't been warned.

A baby will also have soft spots on their head for the first few months, the thought of which, if you're anything like me, might make you feel queasy. These are called fontanelles and are there so the skull could squish up during the birth so your baby could get out and now stay soft for a while so your baby's brain can grow. They may seem fragile and many dads will avoid ever going anywhere near them, but you needn't worry too much. They are well protected by a sturdy membrane so it's OK if they get touched gently. They will get firmer and firmer over time and, by 18 months, they will have completely gone.

The umbilical stump

This is the yuck bit of the umbilical cord that stays attached to your baby's belly and you'll probably just try to ignore it. All you need to do is clean around it regularly and be gentle with it as it gradually dries out then naturally falls off, but keep an eye out for any bleeding or discharge as that could mean it's infected. After a few days it may start to smell bad, but don't worry, it'll be gone soon and you can dropkick that thing into the nearest bin.

Unless, of course, you are one of those people who thinks this type of thing is a keepsake. I know a few people who have held on to the umbilical cord and I have given their names to the police. I just don't get it. At what point would you get that out of the memories box and reminisce? What will your kid think? What would *you* do if the next time you went to your dad's house, he got out a dried-up tube that used to connect you to the inside of your mum to look at and pass around and share stories about? Would you think that's normal or would you think it's really, really weird? Exactly.

VISITORS

Some family members will come and see your new baby in hospital, but they discourage too many visitors on the ward. At first, I thought it was nice that families visited and wondered why they'd restrict it, then the woman across from my wife had parents, brothers, sisters, nieces, nephews and cousins all visit at once to enjoy a chippy tea and I decided it's not nice at all and it should be banned. But whether it's at the hospital or your home when you get back, everyone will probably want to see your baby as soon as they can.

It's hard to know how to handle visitors in those first few days. You might have several different friendship groups and sections of the family (maybe divorced parents, step-parents, and so on), so you'll be conscious of not upsetting one set or showing favouritism. The result could be an endless stream of visitors to host, often bringing presents you have to find a place for or flowers, which at this point just feel like another bloody thing to look after. While you might just be able to manage the role of host, it's a lot to ask of your partner. You've been through loads, but she's been through fifty times as much. She hasn't slept properly for months, she has just had a traumatic medical procedure, and now she has been thrust into motherhood, trying to learn everything a mum needs to know (RIGHT NOW) to keep her baby alive.

While visitors will understandably want to just cuddle the baby and eat biscuits, your partner is dealing with the huge stress of coping as a mother and maybe getting to grips with trying to breastfeed (which she probably doesn't feel 100 per cent comfortable doing in front of Great Uncle Tony). It also takes up valuable time you both really need for sleeping.

A good technique I've heard some people use is to ask all of your guests to bring some food with them. Then, when they arrive, tell them to make the cups of tea. They won't mind at all and it eases the workload for you. But don't feel a pressure to have visitors straight away because you think everyone does or you don't want to upset the people visiting. It's highly likely you are worrying about nothing. Your family are obviously excited to see you all, but they will absolutely understand if you need a bit of time to settle in, recharge and make sure the baby is OK before they visit. And if they don't, fuck 'em.

It feels a bit full-on at first, but the visitors will stop quite quickly. Seeing your baby once is enough for most people. And you'll notice a huge difference if you go on to have a second or third child. Those people who had to see your first kid as soon as possible will get their fill from liking a picture on Facebook.

SAFER SLEEP

It can be very tempting to put your baby in your bed with you. It's a lovely feeling to have them all cuddled up and, for some babies, it seems like the only thing that will soothe them. But you shouldn't. We had the dilemma when our baby grew to an enormous size at an alarming rate, so no longer fitted in his Moses basket. And the crib we had for him didn't look big enough, so we briefly discussed letting him stay in our bed for the night. We decided against it, because we were far too worried that there might be some rolling in the night and he might crush us.

In all seriousness, as lovely as the idea might seem, almost all experts warn against letting your baby share your bed. You are introducing too many dangerous variables compared to their cot or crib. It might seem like a small risk to you, but it's one that just isn't worth taking.

What to put in the crib or cot

As little as possible. A fitted sheet, a breathable blanket, a baby sleeping bag, your baby – and that's it. You might really want to put that super cute teddy in there, but there's no point in risking it. It will make the cot more dangerous and a baby really doesn't give a shit about teddies at this point. If you like it so much, you can always put it in your bed. You might also be tempted by cot bumpers because they look like something that will make the cot safer, but they are a big suffocation risk. I'll hand over to Dr Adam Kay to make it clearer:

ADAM KAY: I'd probably be stripped of my ambassadorial duties for The Lullaby Trust if I didn't take this opportunity to talk about safer sleep advice to reduce the risk of sudden infant death syndrome (SIDS). Always put your baby on their back to sleep, make sure they live in a smoke-free environment, have them sleep in a separate cot but in the same room as you for the first six months and use a firm, flat, waterproof mattress. Don't sleep on a sofa or armchair with your baby, don't sleep in the same bed – especially if you're knackered or have been smoking, drinking or taking drugs. Never cover your baby's face or head or use loose bedding, and don't let your baby get too hot.

You should also keep an eye on the room temperature – between 16 and 20°C is safe for sleeping babies. Adam mentioned The Lullaby Trust and I highly recommend their website (lullabytrust.org.uk) as a resource for everything to do with safe sleeping for babies.

HOLDING IT

Most men hold their baby like it is going to explode. It might. But only in a way that will cause a mess in its nappy or on your

T-shirt. A baby is a lot more robust than you probably imagine (just think about what it went through during the birth), so relax – it will make your body softer, so the baby will be comfier and it will all feel a lot easier. Babies' heads loll about a lot because they don't have the strength to hold them up yet, so you should support them in the crook of your arm or upright on your chest and make sure to support their head and neck when transferring them into a car seat/crib/nervous uncle's arms.

You will gradually get more and more confident with this and, within a week, you'll look like you've been doing it forever, then you'll be able to feel smug in front of all your mates who are as hopeless as you were a few days ago.

It goes without saying, but keep hot drinks well away and don't drink them while you are holding the baby, even if you think you are being careful. This will mean lots of your cups of tea go cold, but unfortunately this is an unavoidable part of being a parent and you've just got to learn to like cold tea. Or you can do what my wife does and put it in the microwave. But I've always found that very unnatural and not something I'm personally comfortable with.

DRESSING IT

This is so much more complicated than you could have imagined. You are familiar with all of the component parts of the baby – arms, legs – it's standard stuff. But they don't all work in the way you'd expect them to and they feel like they're made of jelly. It's like trying to put an octopus into a pair of tights.

Once they are in their babygrow, you need to fasten everything up. Press studs are one of those things that, in your imagination, seem simple. But in practice, they are unbelievably confusing – about 20 tiny metal circle things that all look exactly the same on a wriggly little body and you have to match them all up while the person they are attached to doesn't want you to. You will get it wrong so many times. Some of them have what I call 'dad studs'. It's the little pair of studs they put in the most confusing area of the outfit that are a different colour to all of the others. And you connect these two to help make some sense of the chaos. I don't know why they don't make every pair matching colours. They clearly overestimate dads.

The clothes are a minefield too. If you can, stay out of it. Of all of the aspects of being a dad, this could be the one to cause you the most regular confusion. It's a task you'd think would be pretty simple, having dressed yourself for a few decades. But that's what makes it so infuriating. You should be able to do it, but you just can't.

Baby clothes don't follow the same rules as ours, you see. You can't just stick them in jeans and a T-shirt because fashion is different for kids. If you put them in the stuff we wear, it looks like they are in fancy dress. They also have different rules on layers and even some items that adults don't wear. It's close to what we do, but there are enough differences to make it bewildering for the new dad.

There have been times when I've felt bad because I've been very aware that I am playing into a sexist stereotype that Mum dresses the kids, so I've really tried. At points I've been certain that I've cracked it and I've cockily wandered into the room where my wife is, laid out my outfit choice, smiled, closed my eyes and waited for my praise. After a moment of silence, I've opened them to see my wife looking at the clothes as if I've just presented her with a family of voles.

There's always something I can't quite get right. It might be the way I've matched the colours or the combination of layers. I might pick what I think is a dress and it turns out it's just a top. Or what I think is a hat and it turns out to be a sock.

DAD TRICK When it comes to dressing your child, play within your ability and don't try getting creative. Focus on the next three to five outfits that the baby's mum dresses them in and memorize them. Write down a description of them or even draw them if you need to. Then, just pick one of these each time you find yourself dressing the kid. The chances are you won't do it every day, so that should be just enough variation for it to seem like you know what you're doing. Mum might even forget that she has assembled that outfit before and think she's had a baby with Gok Wan. When she's impressed by your outfit choice, just smile and say, 'I guess I've just got an instinct for style,' then swagger off in your jogging bottoms and Oasis T-shirt.

POSTNATAL CHECKS

Midwives – and, later, health visitors – will visit you fairly regularly after the birth to see if Mum and baby are doing OK. And don't worry, they won't care that your house is an absolute tip at this point. Everyone's is. They will do checks on the mum to make sure she's recovering well from the birth and on the baby for any signs of infection or jaundice, which is quite common in newborns. They'll also do a heel prick test (the newborn blood spot test) and will monitor your baby's weight.

Your baby might lose up to 10 per cent of their body weight in the first few days, which is quite alarming if you didn't know that beforehand. I didn't know that beforehand. But it's completely normal and fine as long as they start to put it back on after a few days and, if they don't, the medical professionals will intervene.

As it happened, our son didn't start putting weight back on. In fact, he was losing more. And when you have something already so tiny and fragile, losing more than a tenth of their weight is worrying. We also noticed he was very jittery. After a few checks, they found his sodium was low and he was dehydrated, so they decided that it'd be best to get him checked at the hospital. It is brilliant that this happens so quickly to help out your baby, but let me tell you, this is the last place you want to go at this point. When you drive away from the hospital with your baby that first time, you hope that is you done until they break their arm falling off the trampoline you'll inevitably have to buy them in a few years.

At the hospital, they did lots of tests, then told us they'd need to keep him in until he started to put on weight. The mixture of feelings here is hard to describe. You have the reassurance that the professionals are stepping in to help, but just being on a children's ward makes you feel like you're in a situation that isn't good and you can't help but feel like you've failed to care for your child properly.

It's at this point you realize that nothing else in life really matters apart from your child's health. In our case, we stayed in hospital for a few days and they put my son on an intensive feeding regime, like De Niro training for his role as Jake LaMotta in *Raging Bull*. (But unless I've misremembered it, De Niro didn't do it on my wife's breast milk.) For those few days, my wife was constantly connected to either our baby or a breast pump as we slept on a camp bed surrounded by smiling cartoon characters painted on the wall which, by day three, were nightmarish because they were all just a little bit off (they had given Mickey Mouse nostrils). I felt absolutely drained and I hadn't done anything compared to my wife, who was being literally drained for every waking hour. I was even more in awe of what a mum does instinctively for their kid. Man, we've got it easy.

Thankfully, my son started to gain weight. It turned out he just needed a bit of a kick-start and he remained a healthy (and chunky) baby from then on. It's an example of how lucky we are to have the amazing people of the NHS and how, even though it feels worrying when they intervene, your baby will get the help they need to get back to fighting fitness as quickly as possible.

CHAPTER 6
THE FIRST MONTH

I've heard a lot of people say that the first few weeks and months are the hardest. And I suppose there are a lot of moments that feel really difficult, but that's mainly because of the worries you have. Once you learn to deal with the stuff in your head, there are actually a surprising number of moments when you can take it easy. I didn't fully realize it at the time, but now I look back on those first months and can't believe how much we could sit around and watch Netflix (admittedly, some of it in the middle of the night). You have a baby who sleeps for 16 hours a day, no one is bothering you because they assume you haven't got a second to spare and the baby is too young to hold any influence on the viewing choices. If you really focus, you can get through a serious amount of TV series in those first months. I have such fond memories of those early days. Lots of cuddles, daytime naps, relaxed long walks, but mainly watching Walter White's crystal meth business flourish. The memories do blur sometimes though and I'll find myself recalling my baby in a gunfight with Heisenberg, which I'm 90 per cent sure didn't happen.

The truth is, nature is way too clever to just pile on all of the demands of being a parent straight away. Instead, it slowly eases you in. There is a fable called 'the boiling frog', which describes how a frog complies with being boiled alive. The premise is that if a frog is put suddenly into boiling water, it will jump out, but if the frog is put in tepid water which is then brought to a boil slowly, it's so gradual it will not realize the danger and will be cooked to death. You are the boiling frog, mate. But this early bit is the part that is like a nice warm bath, so enjoy it!

BONDING WITH YOUR BABY

Bonding can be hard for the dad because you're starting from scratch while the mum has been bonding with the baby for the entire pregnancy. Mums are very sneaky like that. So, you'll possibly feel like your relationship isn't as strong as theirs at first, but that's fine.

You probably had something in your head about the way a father would bond with his kid. Maybe you'd imagined watching the football together, having a beer, not talking too much but letting them know that you love them with the odd ruffle of the hair and approving smile. Well, that's not exactly how it goes. Bonding in the first stages of your baby's life is often just holding them close. Touch is one of the most important senses for the newborn baby, so give loads of cuddles, hold them when they cry and do plenty of skin-to-skin, like you did after the birth. All of these little things will become the stuff that makes your baby feel safe. Chat to them too. They won't be listening to the words, not because your words are boring, but all they care about is the soothing tone and rhythm of your voice. At the moment your baby just sees you as a blob, not because of all the biscuits you've been eating, but because they don't really see people, just shapes, and yours is a nice, familiar one. And they will also recognize your smell, not because of all the showers that you haven't taken, but because it's one of the most familiar smells to them and it will make them feel safe.

Thinking about it, you can actually do all this while watching the football and having a beer. So maybe the version in your head was pretty accurate after all.

Eventually, the interaction picks up a bit and you'll start smiling, babbling and laughing with one another, but that can take a few months. So, until then, prepare for this relationship to be a bit one-sided. That's OK though; everything you are doing now is laying the groundwork for later and will make them feel safe and comforted by you for the rest of their life. Put in the work early on and you'll be rewarded in old age when they let you move in with them after you've lost your faculties.

When your baby is a few months old you can start playing

around with them a lot more. Bouncing, rolling around, tickling, throwing a baby up in the air (and catching it) are all classic dad activities. This kind of fast, risky play that dads always seem to love is actually great for your baby because it releases oxytocin, endorphins and dopamine. It helps them develop their coordination, mental resilience and social skills too. Just be careful, the chances of you getting a head to the face or a knee to the balls are dangerously high. Even though physical play is fun, try not to become one of those dads you see in pubs, holding up their hands for their kid to punch. Oh, and don't drop them. And if you do drop them, don't tell Mum. She'll ban the bonding.

DAD TRICK Tense up your lips when playing with your infant. They have a tendency to throw their heads directly at your mouth every now and again. As silly as you'll feel pouting like Mick Jagger, you'll look sillier without a front tooth.

ELIS JAMES: When Isy was about six months' pregnant with our first child, I was backstage at a gig and told one of the other acts. Rather than the usual 'Oh, congratulations', he said, 'Don't worry if you don't bond with your baby immediately. My son is two now and I'd like to spend every second of the day with him if I could, but that took eighteen months.' No one had ever said anything like that to me before, and it was actually very reassuring. It's really easy to worry that parenthood comes completely naturally to everyone else and not you, so it was a huge relief to discover that other parents had their own concerns and problems.

TWINS (AND MULTIPLE BIRTHS)

When things got especially stressful in those early days, I'd always reassure myself by saying, 'Imagine what it must be like having twins.' But then I stopped needing to imagine, because I asked my friend, Jen Brister. It sounds pretty full-on.

JEN BRISTER: If you have one baby and there are two of you and you think you are overwhelmed, imagine adding another baby into the mix, and that's what it's like having twins.

I need to be clear that I am so grateful that we have our two boys – the advantages, at least for a lezza couple like us, is that, in terms of IVF, we got a two-for-one deal. Great savings were made. If you only want two children, then twins, in many ways, is perfect. They're six now and they play really well together, they're best mates and they can often amuse themselves, which is a bonus.

The flip side of that is that for the first two years at least, in every other way it's fucking horrific. It's literally twice the work and half the sleep.

Also, travelling anywhere with twins requires immense organization. If you go away for more than one day you have to pack with military precision. You can't wing this shit. I know this all too well after leaving the house without any spare nappies and having to wrap my son's bum in my jumper. (No, I don't have that jumper anymore.)

The other problem I wasn't anticipating is the endless small talk you have to suffer with strangers. You'd think people had never seen a couple of babies before. Other parents are the worst: 'Oh my God, they're so adorable! I have a son and a daughter, they're 28 and 24 now; they've both graduated from university and have great jobs!' All parents do it – they have to tell you they have kids and then give you their CV: 'Not only did I have children, I have two successful ones which means that I'm a shit-hot mum and winning at life...anyway, good luck with these two.' I'm sure that's not how it's meant, but what the hell am I supposed to say to that? 'That's wonderful! My son just learned to hold a cup so we'll be on the blower to Mensa any day now.'

The other lot who can't get enough of us is basically any human-type person who has ever met a twin: 'My mum is a twin!', 'I'm a twin', 'I have twins!', 'My favourite movie is Twins!' What are you supposed to do with that information? 'That's great to hear, thanks for letting us know...OK, BYE NOW.'

If you're reading this and you do have twins and are currently thinking you'll never survive this time, YOU WILL. And in the long term it pays off. Particularly when your mate has just had their second baby (and, unlike their first, this one doesn't sleep a bloody wink) and they're crying into their coffee/pint/wine/gin/water, you can be that empathetic ear while also high-fiving the fact that your kids sleep through the night.

Who's smug now, sucker?

DADMIN

Here are a few practical things you need to know about in the early days:

The red book

This is a little book with a red plastic cover and it's the thing you will need for every baby appointment for the foreseeable future. It's a way of each medical professional logging the information about your baby correctly, otherwise they'd have to rely on you to relay it:

'So, Dad, tell me all about your baby.'

'He's a boy and, umm, yep, quite little at the moment…but, umm…getting bigger…seems like a nice guy…'

No one wants that, so keep the red book safe.

Registering the birth

Some families like to do this together. (But it might be a bit of a let down if you're expecting an occasion. It's just admin.) Some see it as a classic dad job. It gets you out of the house, you have to go to a place, fill in a form and pay a set amount of money. Easy. Or so you might think. But when you are sitting in the office at the town hall being quizzed on the mum's birthday and the chosen spelling of your new kid's name, you better make sure you have your facts straight. Because all of this stuff is going to be written on the birth certificate forever. If the mum thinks you are spelling your kid's name 'Harriett', with two ts, and you have spelled it 'Keith', with one t, there's going to be hell to pay.

So, here's the stuff you need to know:

- Place and date of birth of the baby.
- Sex of the baby (if you're unsure about this one, do a quick penis check before you leave the house).
- Name of the baby (triple-check the spelling).
- Yours and the mum's full name and address.
- Yours and the mum's date of birth.
- Yours and the mum's place of birth.
- Date of your marriage or civil partnership.*
- Job titles of both parents.
- The mum's maiden name.

---

* If you're not married, the mum has to be the one to go and do this task. So if you really want to get out of the house on this errand, get down on one knee, quickly.

And the stuff you need to take with you:

- Proof of ID.
- The baby's red book (where all of the medical info is).
- Your debit card because it costs just over a tenner to buy the birth certificate.

It has to be done within the first twenty-one days in Scotland and the first six weeks in England, Wales and NI or your baby will not technically exist. Which can make it hard for them to rent a car. You don't want that.

THE FEAR

In the first stages of fatherhood, you will be totally scared all the time. You know that feeling when you first get an iPhone and it's so beautiful and precious, you are convinced you are going to break it? Well, your new baby is like that (and, by coincidence, it will also be the one to break your iPhone).

Everything about them is fragile. Everything makes you worry. They breathe in a way that looks and sounds completely unnatural. It's fast and irregular, about 40–50 breaths per minute, and they will speed up and slow down in a way that keeps your blood pressure at dangerously high levels.

There's no way to avoid worrying, and telling you to just stop immediately is as effective as telling you to just stop producing red blood cells. But try not to worry about how much you are worrying. It's a demonstration of your love for this little thing and lays the foundations for how much you will care for it its entire life. You won't always have these levels of anxiety. Once your body and mind have found a rhythm, everything will be a lot more relaxed. Ask anyone who has more than one kid. With the first, you don't blink in case something happens to them when your lids are shut. With the second, you'll forget what room you've left them in half the time.

Postnatal depression

I know this isn't something you want to be thinking about, but it's an incredibly common problem and recognizing it in your partner (or yourself) can only make things better, faster. It affects more than 1 in 10 mums and can affect dads too. The good news is that most people make a full recovery and it doesn't affect the future relationship with your child.

It is your job to look out for it in your partner. It can be tricky because the first stages of parenthood are an incredibly emotional time anyway. You will have heard of what they call 'the baby blues', which is when the mum feels anxious, tearful and generally low after giving birth. This is unbelievably common, but will only normally last a couple of weeks. If you notice that your partner has these symptoms for longer than that or they start later, it could be postnatal depression (PND).

PND can start any time within the first year after your child's birth and other symptoms include difficulty bonding with the baby, lack of enjoyment in the wider world, no energy, withdrawing contact from other people and frightening thoughts (for example, hurting the baby).

It is not your fault or your partner's if PND develops. It is an illness like any other. Seeking help won't mean your baby will be taken away from you, it will just mean the mum is helped to recover as quickly as she can.

An incredibly moving book about life with PND is *Something to Live For* by Laura Canty. It can be a difficult subject to read about, but the more we learn and talk about it, the fewer people will have to suffer with it alone.

SLEEP (YOU)

Sleep is one of the most popular topics of conversation for new parents. They talk about sleep so much that non-parents often enter into it while listening. I used to think they just spoke about it because their lives had become so boring that's all they had. And while that might be the case, you have to understand that the obsession with sleep has developed because they are experiencing such an extreme lack of it and they realize just how much they need it. Sleep is essential to keep you functioning and maintain your sanity. Without it, your mood would be all over the place, and your level of performance would slow down to that of a 20-year-old laptop that has streamed too many illegal football matches.

Even though it's tough, there's something quite nice about realizing what your essential needs are. I've heard ex heroin addicts say that one thing they miss about their life on heroin is the simplicity, because when you're an addict, you forget all about the trivial concerns of everyday life. There are only ever two things on your to-do list: 'Get heroin' and 'Take heroin'.

That's what it's like with sleep.

So, if you're finding the conversations about sleep boring and hard to empathize with before you've had the baby, try doing this: every time you hear the word 'sleep', imagine they are saying the phrase 'a bit of heroin'. Not only will it help you understand the serious need, it will also make your friends seem a lot more interesting. ('Craig has to have a bit of heroin on the bus to work so he can get through the morning.')

But there will be times when you inevitably don't get enough sleep and, if you are anything like me, you will start to obsess about how little you're getting and convince yourself it's going to kill you. Well, don't worry, the chances are it will just slowly destroy your mind rather than make you instantly drop dead. And as nice as sleep is, people can survive on very little. Margaret Thatcher famously ran the country on only four hours a night, so, if nothing else, you should have the energy to get up and give your baby milk. Then snatch it back again. Then crush any kind of baby union your kid is thinking of forming.

IAIN STIRLING: Not sleeping was the main thing I was worried about. I fucking love sleep. I've been sacked from jobs, been late to doctor's appointments and missed out on countless free hotel breakfasts. It's so great. Whenever I chatted to a parent they always said 'sleep now'. They were smiling when they said it, but there was a terror in their eyes that always made me worry. Sometimes I had to take a quick nap just to get over it.

SLEEP (BABY)

Your new baby will be nocturnal because when they were in the womb, the mum moving around in the day rocked them to sleep and the stillness of the night made them bored, restless and awake. In hindsight, it would have been better if, during the pregnancy, my wife had stayed completely still during daylight hours and hit the treadmill from dusk till dawn. Maybe next time.

You can encourage your baby to adjust to a normal sleep pattern by keeping their Moses basket (or whatever they sleep in) in a bright area with normal levels of noise during the day and in your dark, quiet, comfy bedroom at night. You can use something to play white noise if need be (Ewan the Dream Sheep is a popular choice) to remind them of being in the womb – the good old days.

As time goes by and your baby grows, it's good to try to establish a consistent bedtime routine. Doing the same thing each night, for instance a bath, then a feed, then a story, then bed (obviously this changes a bit, depending on the child's age), can really help ensure your baby goes to bed relaxed and has a good night's sleep because they know exactly what is happening and feel comforted by the routine.

There are plenty of more structured sleep-training methods out there and a lot of parents choose one to follow before they even have their baby. Often it's because they know other new parents who have told them that this method is the *absolute best* and always works. It's worth doing a bit of research because you might find the one that works perfectly for you and you can then be the new parent who tells everyone they meet about the *absolute best* method. But it's also very likely you'll find all of the schools of thought contradictory and, ultimately, that none of them work. Don't worry about that because each baby is different and most parents just end up working it out as they go.

A newborn will sleep for anywhere between eight and eighteen hours a day for the first three months. Don't go planning a night out just yet, though, because it will be divided up into loads and loads of short naps throughout the day and night, with regular waking for feeds.

Between three and six months you'll notice they (hopefully) start sleeping more at night than during the day, and the night sleeps will total eight hours or more with fewer wakes to feed. The official advice is to still keep your baby sleeping in your bedroom at night until at least the six-month mark (see page 115 for more on safer sleep).

From one year onwards your baby will sleep for between twelve and fifteen hours a day. Most of it will be at night, but they will probably still have one or two naps during the day that will gradually phase out over the next year and a half (and you will really miss them when they are gone because it's the only time you can get anything done). A lot of babies will be in their own room by this age as well.

You'll hear a lot – and think a lot – about the point when you can get your baby to 'sleep through', which is what other smug parents call it when their baby sleeps through the whole night without waking. Even though this will feel like the thing you want more than anything you have ever wanted, you don't. Despite what the bags under your eyes are saying, it wouldn't be good if this happened too soon because your baby needs to be feeding regularly day and night to keep growing and developing in a healthy way.

It feels like it's the luck of the draw with how well your baby sleeps. I've got mates whose kids need perfect silence and others whose kids need white noise played all night. Even my own two kids are completely different. My daughter is a light sleeper who will wake every now and again, but silently settle herself. My son is an incredibly deep sleeper, who wakes up and yells several times a night. When the girl gets up in the morning, she is full of the joys of life. When the boy wakes up, he looks like a shift worker with a drink problem.

No matter how they are in general, though, you'll definitely have good and bad nights. There will be plenty of times you have to rock them to sleep, put them down incredibly carefully and sneak out like a ninja. There will be times when you are in there rocking your baby and it feels like it is never going to end. I find the best way to deal with this is to use a technique I once heard an ex-prisoner talk about. He had spent most of his life in an American jail for a crime he didn't commit, but said he managed to deal with it by just going elsewhere in his head. So, every day he would visit somewhere from his past or explore somewhere new via his mind. Now every time one of my kids won't sleep and I have to stand there holding them, I don't mind because I'm watching Oasis at Knebworth.

RUSSELL KANE: I was an absolute sleep Nazi. I made my wife agree to my regime before I even agreed to start trying for a baby. Luckily, we were both on the same page.

And it's easy. A baby needs to sleep for about 16 hours, so just keep them awake in the day and they will sleep longer at night. If my daughter slept a minute longer than she was supposed to, I woke her up. If she got too sleepy, I'd entertain her or put a wet flannel on her feet. We got sleep nailed. We were on eight hours by eight weeks and twelve hours by twelve weeks. It's when the eyes flip open that the hell starts.

ELIS JAMES: Our eldest was one of those incredible babies who needed to be woken to be fed and slept from 8pm until 8am no matter where we were, how noisy it was or how disrupted her routine had been. In an amazing act of hubris, we decided that this was down to how brilliant we were as parents and that, if everyone else could follow our example, the world's sleep epidemic would be cured and we could all move on with our lives, refreshed. This proved to be absolute nonsense and, when our son was born four years later, we had over a year of getting up multiple times a night, and his usual waking time was eye-wateringly early until he was 22 months old. I will never claim credit for anything positive in my life ever again.

A NEW PATTERN

Unless you're a milkman, you are going to be getting up a lot earlier than you used to. Now, you could look at this as a negative because you're not getting the sleep you feel you need, your day is going to be ruined by tiredness and the only TV programmes that are on at 5am are reruns of *Changing Rooms* from the nineties, so the 'after' shots look like the 'before' shots and the 'before' shots make you want to cry.

Or you could look at the positives. You have an extra four hours you didn't have before. After you've sorted milk, breakfast, changing, and so on, you could use it constructively. Maybe make a start on that novel you've been planning to write, or work on your child's language skills, or stick a podcast on, or finally watch *The Wire*, or scroll through TikTok for hours, confused.

This new schedule will have knock-on effects, though. You are now existing on a different plane than you ever have before. You'll end up doing that thing you do when you come back from a holiday abroad, saying, 'I know it's 11am, but it's 4pm for me.' You'll start eating at bizarre times. If you're getting up at 5am instead of 8am then you're having your lunch at 10am instead of 1pm and your tea at 3.30pm. It all contributes to the feeling that your new life is some blurry fever dream.

You'll appreciate the pleasure of an early night more than ever before. Not a 'wink wink' early night, but a 'quick, sleep!' early night. Because you have no idea when the baby is going to get up, you can never be sure how early is too early to go to bed. If they get up at 7am and don't wake in the night, an 11pm sleep will give you your recommended eight hours. But let's see what happens when we add in a few variables: A restless night? Three feeds? The time it takes to get back off to sleep after each disruption? What if they wake up at 5am instead of 7am? You're suddenly down to four hours, mate! So, to be on the safe side, it's best to get into bed straight after *Countdown* finishes.

While we're on the subject, don't ever make the mistake of waking up and saying, 'They were good in the night, weren't they?' because you are setting yourself up for the reply, 'No. They were awful. But you slept through the whole thing.' If you think it's been a good night, keep quiet. Wait for her to tell you. Then try to resist lying and saying, 'No. They were awful. But you slept through the whole thing.'

BATH TIME!

Bathing your baby can be a really happy time. Maybe it's because you get to see your little one splashing about with a huge smile on their face. Or because throwing them into a completely different situation (don't throw them) can often make them more excitable and giggly. Or because there is just something incredibly cute and funny about a baby's bare, squishy bum. Or maybe it's because it's the last big task of the day and you know that the moment it finishes, you can open that bottle of wine.

When your baby is very little, you'll probably bathe it in the baby bath, but it's a good idea to put the little bath inside your main bath because it's easy to underestimate just how much water that little person can transfer from the bath to anywhere other than the bath. We first did it in our living room and, within a minute or two, it looked like the lower deck of the *Titanic*.

You'll need to fill the bath with water and use a thermometer to make sure it's warm, but not too hot. Plain water is best, though, let's be honest, we all put a bit of bubble bath in (the ones especially designed for babies are best because they are kinder to their sensitive skin). Slowly lower your baby in, preparing yourself that they might hate it and immediately thrash around like a trout on a boat. They will hopefully get used to it as you do it more regularly, but I'm not making any promises.

You might get lucky though. Some babies really like it straight away and, if they do, baths at this stage are quite a quick job. Just pop them in, sponge clean them, play a little bit, wash their hair if you need to (again, use shampoo that is designed for babies), then take them out and snuggle them up in a soft towel until they are dry.

When your kid gets old enough, you'll transfer to the big bath. There are a couple of main differences here. For a start, there's a lot more water in it, so there will be a lot more water coming out of it. The first time in the big bath, you'll feel like Lieutenant Dan on the ship in *Forrest Gump*, so make sure the sealant in your bathroom is up to scratch and wear a mac. The other main difference is that the big bath isn't curved to support them sitting up, so at first you're going to have to get a bath seat or support, or keep hold of them to stop them sliding around. You'll need to bend right over the bath to do this, which means you get to watch their smiling face as you feel one of the discs in your back slip. You're making beautiful memories that you will be reminded of every time you get up out of a chair and feel a twinge in your spine.

To help make sure they continue to enjoy bath time (because your life will be so much easier if they do), try to make the bathroom lovely and warm, warm their towel and, when they get out, either stand them on a soft bath mat so they don't slip or wrap them up and give them a big cuddle. Sounds nice, doesn't it?

Oh, and maybe it goes without saying, but never, ever leave your baby or young child alone in the bath.

How often?

You don't need to bath a baby every day because they don't really do a lot like adults do. (Have you noticed, you never see a baby carrying furniture?) Two or three times a week is more than enough and you can just wash their face, neck, hands and bottom with cotton wool/a flannel in between (what's known as a 'top and tail') instead. But we tried to give our baby a bath every day early on because we found it helped with the bedtime routine and usually led to a better sleep. While we're on the subject, although a baby doesn't require regular washes, you do. I suspect by this point your general hygiene has dropped to unacceptable levels, so go and have a shower as soon as you can mate. For everyone's sake.

Washing hair

Washing hair is something we expect kids to hate, but I suspect that's because they get shampoo in their eyes one time, then struggle and cry the next time, and from then on the parent just does it as quickly as possible to stop the crying, meaning more shampoo in the eyes. If you try to avoid the negative experience of getting shampoo in their eyes for as long as you can, hopefully you will avoid falling into this cycle for as long as you can too. Try tipping their head back a bit like they do in a salon. You can add to the experience by asking them if they are going anywhere nice on holiday this year.

Babies can often have 'cradle cap' when they are little, which is basically a crusty scalp. Resist the temptation to pick at it if you're the type of person who likes doing that sort of thing. It will usually clear up on its own in a few weeks and is helped along by shampooing. If you want to hurry it up – say, if your baby is heading to a black tie event and is worried about flakes showing up on their shoulders – you can rub a bit of baby oil or vegetable oil on their scalp to help soften the flakes.

Bath toys

Bath toys are fun, but will gradually take over your bathroom. What was once a tranquil place will become overrun by plastic octopuses and goggle-eyed dolphins. You'll never truly be able to relax in the bath again because, even when you close your eyes, you'll know that 30 brightly coloured sea creatures are all staring at you.

Be careful with the squeezy bath toys. Babies love them because they can chew on them and it's funny when you squeeze them and they squirt water, but they are notorious for collecting mould inside. The laughter stops when the squidgy frog spits spores of mould into your baby's face.

CUTTING NAILS

It's something you probably didn't give a second thought to before becoming a dad, but cutting your baby's nails is a very scary task for a new parent. Babies need their nails cutting regularly because they have a tendency to scratch themselves and this can hurt them. But you and your partner will be terrified to do it because everything is really tiny and delicate, so you'll be paranoid you are going to accidentally snip an entire digit off.

Well, first of all, you need to make sure you use nail clippers or scissors that are designed for babies – these are nicely rounded and would be difficult to cause harm with. You can always wait until they are asleep so wriggling is at a minimum. Then, you just need to do what bomb disposal experts do – slow down and regulate your breathing, which will regulate your heartbeat, which will make you calmer as you slowly and carefully neutralize the threat.

THE OUTDOORS

An unexpected perk of fatherhood is how much walking you end up doing. Whether it's to get them to sleep, stop them from crying or keep them entertained, you wander around with your baby a lot and you'll really grow to like it.

When you spend so much time inside, the fresh air can really clear your head, reset yours and your baby's mood and it gives you the sense that you've done something with your day (a feeling you can often find yourself missing when you become a parent). It can be good to get out whatever the weather. Get cold, get wet, get muddy. You can always get warm, dry and clean when you get back home.

When your baby is quite new, this is your opportunity to really go for it. In the first few months, you are basically pushing around a potato in a pram so you can go on adventures, purely for your own entertainment, under the guise of looking after your kid. It doesn't make a difference to your baby if you are doing an educational museum visit or a football shirt exhibition, so take your opportunity, pal. Because before you know it, they start becoming less potato-like and compliant and they will have their own ideas about where would be a good place to go. And their ideas will be shit.

So, why not go sightseeing? Or on a self-curated musical history tour? Or, if you live near the place you grew up, why not do a visit to all of the key places from your youth, then feel really sad all afternoon because the past has gone forever? Or a coffee shop tour. Whatever you're into.

Use the first year to do the big distances, because when they become mobile, you'll notice they move their legs a lot slower than you, and they are tiny compared to yours, so you move at a torturously slow pace and your range of travel becomes minuscule. You can still do sightseeing tours, but the sights will be the houses on the streets next to yours.

DAD TRICK These early days are your time to really discover the joy of the relaxed mid-walk pint. Admittedly, it's a different experience to going to the pub for the night with all the lads, but it is a lovely little dad perk and it's a completely guilt-free drink. No one begrudges you it and it doesn't hinder your ability to parent (as long as you don't go *too* premium). Pick a nice beer, take your time and enjoy it. And when you arrive back home, you take all of the glory of looking after the baby all afternoon.

Baby-changing facilities

It's an inevitable fact that sooner or later you'll be out and about and your baby will shit. So, you have to find somewhere to change them. Most places have changing facilities, which is good. There aren't many more good things to be said about them.

Firstly, a lot of them are locked, so you'll have to wander around the bar or restaurant with your shat-their-pants baby, trying to find the bloke with the key, who is never around. Or, if the room isn't locked, you'll walk in and realize why it should be when you see the *Racing Post* on the floor and the hell that has been unleashed in the toilet by several tradesmen already that day.

It's best to assume that they will be absolutely awful. That way, you won't be too shocked when they are just slightly worse than that. It's hard for me to accurately describe them because I've blocked out the memories as a coping mechanism. But they look like where you might imagine prisoners of war are put when their captors are particularly unhappy with them. The only silver lining is that you and your baby will both hate them as much as each other, so it might bring you closer, in the way ex-military personnel often have an unbreakable bond because they've seen such terrible things together that no one else could ever understand.

The small bit of justice is that the pleasantness of facilities is inversely proportional to the pleasantness of the place you are in. If you are in a shopping centre, you'll find they have often made much more of an effort to create a nice changing environment, which you need when suffering the hell of shopping. At the other end of the scale, the ones in pubs look the most like terrorist holding cells; strip-lit and cold, with a hard, plastic baby shelf and an overflowing shit bin. They are possibly the bleakest rooms you'll ever go in. So, you might want to make sure you've had a couple of pints first.

HOW TO DEAL WITH CRYING (BABY)

You've probably noticed that babies cry a lot. It's something I was really worried about before becoming a dad, because I found the sound really hard to listen to when I heard it in public and didn't know what I'd do when there was one in my house doing it non-stop. Well, for a start, it's a bit different when it's your own baby. The cry doesn't annoy you in the same way. It just makes you want to make things better for them.

It also helps a lot when you realize that crying isn't the same as it would be for you or me. They're not necessarily sad, they just have quite basic communication skills right now. So, crying is just the universal request for assistance. It could mean, 'Dad, I've got trapped wind and it's really painful! Help me to get it out now!' or it could mean, 'Excuse me pal, I don't suppose there's any more of that milk going is there?' or it could mean, 'I've just seen a fly! What the fuck is a fly?!'

The good thing is that their needs are simple at this point, so 95 per cent of their crying will be because of one of four things: they are hungry, they need changing, they are tired or they are uncomfortable. You'll soon get to know the difference between the cries and then you'll be able to help them more quickly (and so the crying won't last as long), although it's highly likely your partner will tune into their language a lot quicker than you will, and that's to be expected. I know I felt like my wife could speak A-level Baby, while I was still trying to wrap my head around the first line of the phrase book.

As with all of your baby's extreme displays of emotion, try not to get too frustrated or upset. You won't always manage that and sometimes it will feel like the crying will never stop. But it will. Breathe deeply and act calmly. This will help them to do the same.

You will have your happy little baby back in no time. And – I'm aware how soppy this sounds – when your baby is happy, everything feels well in the world.

HOW TO DEAL WITH CRYING (YOU)

I had no idea how emotional I'd be after becoming a dad. I actually thought it would go the other way and, the moment I became a father, I'd click into that distant stoicism you often see in dads on TV. I'd learn to bottle everything up in a completely unhealthy way, until I suffered a nice manly heart attack in my fifties. But no, it was as if the birth busted the floodgates wide open and now I find myself in tears much more than I used to. Some of it is understandable, like when I see something bad happen to a kid on a TV show or watch one of the sad bits on Comic Relief. That's fine and probably quite a healthy thing. But about a month after my son was born, I found myself welling up during an episode of *Take Me Out*.

When you become a dad, you suddenly have all of these

different feelings, some that you haven't felt for decades and some that you've never felt before, so you'll get a bit wobbly every now and then and it can all spill over. Don't worry though, it'll settle down. You might never get back to your old numb self and you'll probably always now be closer to your emotions, but within a few months, you should be able to see a girl decide it's a 'No likey' without breaking down.

RETURNING TO WORK

After your baby has been around for a couple of weeks, it's likely one of you will return to work and the other will become the full-time parent. Even though things are changing, the odds are it will be you who returns to work. This can lead to a lot of misunderstanding, jealousy and resentment, as well as plenty of muttering 'you fucking kidding me?' under your breath. It's understandable, because it's a brand-new situation and you both can't really imagine what the other is going through. The moment you leave for work, you'll be wishing you could just stay at home and watch TV all day like her and she'll be wishing she could just go out and hang out with her mates all day like you. Obviously, that's not what either of you are doing.

You'll struggle to see things from each other's perspectives at first. To her it will seem like you get to just simply slot back into your old life after your fortnight of cuddles; that you've instantly got all that time to yourself, chats with work mates and you get to go to the toilet on your own (if you don't, contact HR).

But you'll think this is totally unfair because you're expected to just go back to doing everything you were doing before with the added weight of all of this new stuff. You have this pressure to provide for your family so they can eat, but you're being made to feel guilty for doing so. And you're not doing it very well because the moment you return home, you're told to take over with the kid, so you're operating on no sleep and it feels like you're failing at everything.

In your most shameful moments, you'll think to yourself, how hard can staying at home all day be? Well, the only way you'll understand is for you to do it. And not one of those 'Daddy days', where you manage to do everything (to prove a point?), because the conditions of those aren't real. It's easy to have a fantastic, productive time with your kid when you know your job ends at the end of the day and you're doing something else tomorrow.

To be a full-time stay-at-home parent is a completely different battle. I thought I had a pretty good idea of what it involved because the nature of my work means I'm around for big chunks of the day. But then someone had sex with a bat and caused a global pandemic and I, like many people, suddenly no longer had much of a job, so experienced what it is like to be a full-time parent. There is a huge difference between what I was doing before (parenting for a few hours, then walking to a coffee shop to write something or driving to a gig) and being Dad full-time. Even though work things aren't always enjoyable (I'm very lucky to have the job I have, but sometimes I have to perform in places like Ramsgate), the fact that your brain and body get to do something different gives you a mental break.

The thing about the job of 'Parent' is it's never-ending.

Unlike other work, where you can achieve things and there's an end point, with parenting often the best you can hope for is to simply maintain. To keep your kid calm, interested and alive for another day.

You are just trying to get from sleep to sleep, then you feel guilty about wishing the time away and not enjoying it like you're supposed to. But your happiness is completely determined by the mood of your kid and they could explode at any moment (mentally or physically). It's never too long until they demand one of their hundreds of feeds or sleeps or burps they seem to need every day and they don't offer anything at all conversation-wise, so you are just talking to yourself all day. You also have all of the other jobs you need to do in the house. If, by some miracle, you manage to keep your baby happy all day, stop the house from going to shit and keep on top of the washing, the big result is…things are the same as they were this morning. Then, tomorrow, the best-case scenario is that it will be the same again.

Then, imagine some prick walking through the door dressed all nicely, with a podcast in his ears and a belly full of delicious street food from that place in town, possibly after a quick post-work pint, asking, 'So, what have you done today?' in a way that is totally loaded with the assumption: 'Not much, right?' Don't you just want to smack him?

It's such a big mental shift to become a full-time parent. You no longer use the parts of your brain you did before and you lose a sense of who you are. Psychologically, that wears you down. So, if you're not the stay-at-home parent, do your best to try to understand and help the one who is. Maybe it's not fair for you, but it's even less fair for them.

These days, having a parent stay at home for an extended period is a luxury, so eventually it's likely you'll both return to work. If your partner returns second, she'll go through all of the dilemmas you did, with the feelings of guilt for not being around and feelings of guilt for enjoying not being around. So, try to help her through it and work out together how best to spend enough time with your kid.

JOSH WIDDICOMBE: Firstly, I should be clear that being a working dad is far easier than being a stay-at-home parent. Now we have that out of the way, the toughest thing I find is getting any time when I am neither working nor parenting. If you are out of the house working you feel so guilty that you are away, the moment you come back you feel you should take over childcare to relieve the pressure on your partner. It would take an astonishing self-confidence (and selfishness) to get back at 6pm and then claim you are too tired to help with bedtime. What this means is there is never a moment when your child is awake when you are neither parenting nor working and, in a strange turn of events, my job is actually now the sweet release from the stress of my life. I never thought I would be living a life where I just had to get through the weekend so that I could have a bit of a relax at work during the week.

DAD TRICK Make your chores work for you. Jobs which were once burdens are now your best friends because they are your ticket to a bit of 'You Time'. Taking bins out is crap, but it's nice and simple. A bin bag isn't going to start crying or need entertaining. Having a bit of head space, regardless of what you're doing, can be exactly what you need, so even something as grim as unclogging the hair from the shower can feel like a trip to a spa. And, even better, you're praised when you've done it. It's the perfect crime. And it's guilt-free because your other half won't care that your motives are selfish. She's enjoyed some nice time without you around and she's also got a shower that doesn't submerge her feet within the first couple of minutes of getting in. Is it depressing that the things that used to be the worst parts of your day are now the best? Best not to think about that.

Working from home

I had an idyllic view that this would be the best of both worlds and I'd get to spend loads of time with the kids as I worked. While that can be true, you need to manage it properly or you just end up feeling guiltier than you would if you were out of the house all day. I would often find myself on my laptop in the corner of the room while my kids played and I'd just feel crap because I could see the kids but I wasn't interacting with them. And I wasn't concentrating on my work either. So I was failing at both things and resenting both things. This isn't any good for your kid either. They can understand it when you leave the house to go and do something. They can't understand you being there but ignoring them and staring at a screen like a robot.

The best solution I've found is to compartmentalize it. If you're working, go somewhere else to work, if possible. Then when you're playing with the kids, throw yourself fully into that and resist checking your phone and emails. Not trying to spread yourself too thinly lets you concentrate on doing each thing properly.

CHAPTER 7

ONE TO THREE MONTHS

The last month has probably been the strangest of your life and the next couple are only going to get slightly more normal. But what is brilliant about the time coming up is that your anxieties are going to settle down, so you can start to enjoy your new baby even more.

The whole thing will feel like a whirlwind right now. Your baby is changing every day and you feel half asleep all the time. But even though it's a challenging period, it's an incredibly special one and there is a lot of fun to be had…

PERKS

Obviously, there's the life-affirming feeling you get when you look into your child's eyes and you're overwhelmed by the greatest and purest love you've ever known. But you don't need me to tell you about all that, what you want from me is the other stuff. The perks no one tells you about. The stuff we keep to ourselves because we don't want to get rumbled. So, let's talk about a few you might have heard about, some you won't have and some, I'm afraid, that I'm going to have to dispel as myths.

Getting girls

A mate of mine once said to me, 'Having kids is great for getting girls.' If you ignore the fact that this is kind of a weird thing to say and you're probably not looking to 'get girls' considering you've just had a kid with someone, I can sort of see his logic. I suppose some women will look at you a bit differently now you have a child because you are demonstrating a quality that most would see as an attractive one. But the attractiveness of your ability to look after a child is probably evened out by the fact that you look like absolute shit all of the time. And even if having a kid did miraculously make you irresistible to women, it's a completely useless superpower; like the story of the daddy-long-legs that contains the most deadly poison in the animal kingdom, but hasn't got the teeth to administer it. And now I think about it, I'm pretty sure that's a myth and they aren't poisonous at all. And now I think about it, there's a chance it isn't lust on the faces of the women who look at you, it's pity. So, I wouldn't suggest having a kid as a wingman. There are much easier ways to be successful with women. I don't know what they are, but there must be.

Positive attention

While a baby isn't going to turn you into Don Juan, it will bring a lot of welcome attention that just makes every day feel a bit brighter. About ten times as many people smile at you than before, which instantly puts you in a better mood. Babies just seem to make people happy, which is nice to see. Then, those people look at you like they think you must be a decent, pleasant person, which is a lovely feeling. It happens mostly with old women, so if you need a bit of a boost, just do a couple of laps of your local bowling green.

Dads get more credit

When you perform normal acts of parenting in a public space, you are treated like a war hero. The same tasks that wouldn't get the mother a second glance have middle-aged ladies fawning over you and the general public rising to give you a standing ovation.

I once cleaned my daughter's face in a coffee shop, while there was also a mother there feeding one of her kids *while* breastfeeding the other. Yet it was me who all of the other customers looked like they were going to start a slow hand clap for. It's completely sexist and unfair, and so hard not to enjoy.

Parking spaces

Let's be honest, this is the reason we all got into fatherhood. All of the stresses of the birth, the tantrums, the lack of a social life, it all melts away when you pull up right by the Aldi entrance and experience the feeling of swinging your car door open to its maximum width.

Unfortunately, like all beautiful things, the world of parent-and-child parking spaces has an ugly side too. You'll start to notice – and get infuriated by – people who park in these spaces when they haven't got kids and, in my experience, they are not cheeky chancers or people with nowhere else to park. They're people (usually men) who hate the thought that anyone might be getting something better than them and they often have faces the colour of boiled ham. Their view (and I know this, because I've had a look at enough online discussions about it to make me lose faith in humanity) is, 'Why should parents get preferential treatment when they *chose* to have kids?' Well, for a start, you bunch of pricks, we didn't all choose it. And, if we did, it wasn't really for the parking spaces (despite what I said earlier). But the main thing here is, the whole point of the special spaces isn't to reward parents, it's to protect everyone. The reason the door opening space is wider is because you need more room to get a kid and a car seat out, so it stops you from bashing up the other cars. And the reason they are so close to the shop is to prevent children having to walk around too much on what is essentially a big square road. Presumably these ham-heads aren't in favour of road traffic accidents. Or maybe they are. Maybe they are exactly the massive wankers they look.

When parking in these spaces out of habit, double-check you've actually got your kid with you or everyone will think you're one of these men.

ENTERTAINMENT FOR BABIES

In the first few months, when humans are at their simplest, the tricks to entertain them are pretty simple too. I learned this to my dismay when I, a professional comedian, tried everything in my arsenal to get a laugh out of my baby and was met with dead-eyed contempt I hadn't seen since a Christmas gig I did in Dartford in 2017. But my wife, who has never even done a five-minute open spot, had him in stitches with – I'm sure she won't mind me saying – some pretty basic material.

This is because babies don't have a particularly discerning taste in comedy at first. That's why you'll see people using the same traditional forms of humour to entertain them: funny voices, raspberries and peekaboo.

If you're looking for a strong, dependable bit of material, by the way, you won't go far wrong with peekaboo and its variants. It has proven time and time again, generation after generation, to be incredibly effective for getting laughs with the under twos.

The technique is simple: all you do is hide your face behind your hands (or a sofa or a door) and your baby will think that one of the most important people in their life has gone forever. There's your jeopardy. Just as they are considering life as an orphan, remove your hand and 'BOO', you're back! Your baby has a rush of adrenaline. It's a mixture of surprise, pure relief and absolute hysterics that your face appeared from nowhere. It's broad humour and it won't win you the Perrier Award, but it'll get a baby laughing, and sometimes you have to just play to the audience you're given. I should've tried it on the Dartford crowd. I bet they would have been rolling in the aisles.

Mobiles are very interesting for babies to look at too, so it's good to have one to hang above their crib or cot. Early on, you should also give your baby regular 'tummy time', which means lying them on their front for short spells to build up the strength in their neck. You can get mats for them to lie on with loads of interesting textures and attachments to keep them entertained.

Baby voice

Sometimes, people speak to babies like they are themselves babies. I used to think this was ridiculous. There was something about that high-pitched babble that I found embarrassing for the person saying it, the baby listening to it and for me, observing the whole silly thing. To me, it was akin to walking up to a dog and talking to it in a gruff 'I'm a dog too' voice. Which I realize some mad bastards do as well.

But I was wrong. I mean, it *is* definitely embarrassing. But it's really good for a baby and there's science to back it up. They tune in to this more sing-song, high-pitched tone. Go on, try it with your kid. Say, 'Who's a cheeky little boy?' in a normal voice and then again in the embarrassing baby voice. If you're in public, you can wait until you get home.

As you can probably guess from the way you felt when I told you to try it just now, a lot of dads won't be comfortable doing it. This means that, if you can stand the shame, it'll put you ahead of most other dads – something I know is important to all of us. But even if you can only bring yourself to do a watered down version, that's not necessarily a bad thing. Some scientists believe the dad's less high-pitched and sing-song voice (their half-arsed self-conscious version) acts as a link to the friendly tones of the baby-speakers and the way people speak in the real world.

You can use that to explain to your partner why you won't do it properly and all your mates will still think you're cool with your manly voice.

Singing

I'm not sure if it's because kids like songs or because you haven't really got anything to say to a baby, but you will end up singing all the time. It will start with the nursery rhymes you half remember from being a kid (and you'll realize just how messed up and death-themed they all are). But soon enough, you will find yourself singing everything: to-do lists, commentaries on mundane activities, passive-aggressive digs at your partner. It's a way of constantly making sounds that are entertaining for your baby. Or a sign you are slowly losing your mind.

After a while you'll start freestyling songs. Here's one of mine from a night when my baby just would not sleep:

(To the tune of *Twinkle, Twinkle, Little Star*)

I should not have been so cheap
Bought a fake Ew-an the Sheep

I've been here for so much time
Will I ever get my wine?

What a stupid prick I am
Stuck in here with Carl the Lamb.

Books

You must quite like them. You're holding one right now. Well – good news – your kid will too. It will be no surprise to you that books are great at developing language and imagination and there are thousands of brilliant children's books to choose from. I recommend the Julia Donaldson ones because they're funny and the rhymes feel really nice to say.

Reading to your child before bedtime is a lovely routine to get into. It's the perfect time to settle down and focus on a nice story and it calms them before bed. No matter what you've been through in the day, this is a chance to end things with a cuddle and a nice shared moment that will make your child feel comforted and loved before they nod off to sleep.

Even very tiny babies like books. You can get special black-and-white contrast ones and ones made of soft material and, when they are a bit older, interactive books with different textures as well as flaps and doors to lift. My advice to you if one of your kid's favourite books is one with doors in it, is to buy a spare because there are only so many times you can repair a ripped cardboard gate before it becomes more tape than cardboard. And my advice to you if you are the author of children's books, is to produce books with little cardboard doors in it. It means parents will have to buy several copies. In hindsight, I should have put some little cardboard doors in this book. Damn.

Parent and baby classes

It's likely you'll have some baby classes available near you. They are everywhere. But it's safe to say that the more middle class the area, the more options you'll have. They generally involve you sitting around in a circle, singing. The chances are it will be mainly mums so your voice will stick out, but get over this and it's really quite nice. Like the early scenes in documentaries on religious cults before all the sexual coercion begins. When I started going to these classes, I made a mental note not to enter into any suicide pacts without checking with my wife first.

They are generally quite welcoming places. All of the parents are going through similar stuff, so the support you give each other is genuinely really valuable. But if you're one of the only dads in a class full of mums, you can't help feeling like the odd one out every now and again. Like when you go for a coffee after the class and they eat cake and say things like, 'After what our bodies have been through, we deserve it!' then glance over at you with your muffin and raise an eyebrow.

Sensory rooms

Before you graduate to the excitement of 'proper' soft play when your kid is a bit older (see page 268), at some centres there's a place you can go when you have a young baby. A calmer, friendlier place, away from the amateur immersive theatre production of *Lord of the Flies* going on in the rest of the building. It's called the 'sensory room' and, when you are in here, it will be the most relaxed you will feel in your fathering career.

For the first time in months, you don't have to watch your baby like a hawk because everywhere is soft and safe. It's dimly lit with hypnotic twinkling and swirling lights projected on the ceiling and glittery relaxing lava-lamp-style lights on the walls. It feels like what heaven might be like. It's almost impossible to tear yourself away from it, but you have to. Because, in your sleep-deprived state, any longer than five minutes in here and you will fall into a slumber so deep that you'll only be woken up when a bearded man is shaking you telling you that you need to get out of here because you are putting off the other parents. And that bearded man is your son. Enjoy the sensory room. But be careful, my friend.

Swimming

You can take your baby swimming from a surprisingly young age and they say that if you get in early enough, their natural reflexes will kick in and they will just instinctively know how to swim. Which is amazing. But, as I learned, not always true.

The first thing to contend with is the awkwardness of the fact that you are probably the only dad and, therefore, the only man standing among a group of women in swimwear. So, you'll need to make sure your eyes always stay above shoulder level. Trying to hold your baby on the surface of the water without looking down will inevitably mean they will get a lot of unexpected dunks, but at least no one will think you're a pervert. Just not a very good dad.

Surprisingly early on, the instructor will encourage you to put your baby underwater and, when they come back up, they will understandably cry. For people who don't like water, babies' eyes produce a lot of it. It's very strange that you've spent months doing everything you can to protect this kid from any discomfort and now you are waterboarding them just because some woman in a swimming cap told you to.

Don't expect your kid to take to it straight away. But you need to be prepared that one kid will and it will make everyone else feel crap. Alfie was his name and I'll remember that baby's smug face till the day I die.

You shouldn't compare kids, but it's hard when you spend most of the lesson trying to stop your baby eating his own hand while Alfie swims past in the background doing the butterfly stroke. You should've seen him. There was a rumour going round that he was in talks for a sponsorship deal with Beats headphones. And I'd never suggest that little Alfie was doping, but I think it'd be in everyone's interests if the baby swimming classes started doing random urine testing. But they won't. And Alfie knew that.

The other annoying thing is, most of the kids were about five months old when we started, but Alfie was only three months. There's nothing more demoralizing than someone younger than you being better than you. And Alfie was over 30 years younger than me.

They will tell you that if your baby gets upset at any point, stop the activity and cuddle. But it gets to the point where it feels ridiculous to call them swimming lessons. They are just long, damp, expensive cuddles.

It's good to remember that you don't need to have the best kid. You just need to not have the worst. So, look to see if there are any babies crying more than yours. If there are, great! If not, that's nothing a little well-directed splash can't help along.

Don't give us all a bad name

Every single time I took my son swimming over the course of several months, the instructor would say, 'Oh, no Mum this week?' Mum had only ever taken him once! I thought, what is her problem with dads? Then, one time, two other dads turned up. Within a couple of minutes of getting in the pool, a competition had started, with each man trying to throw his baby higher in the air than the other (to be avoided, by the way, at least until the baby is six months old). The babies, who were meant to be learning to swim, had become nothing more than pieces of sports equipment. I immediately understood her problem with dads. So, if you can, resist the urge to compete, play or do something stupid in front of the mums, please lads. For all of our sakes.

OTHER PARENTS

It can be tough to make new friends as an adult and you might just think that you don't want to because other parents seem awful. All they want to talk about is the incredibly dull subject of their kid. And they don't seem at all bothered about the incredibly interesting subject of your kid. Or you might think that you don't need to get new mates because you already have a set that you are happy with. But you need to stop seeing them as competitors or potential replacements for your old mates. It's not fair because you've whittled those other friends down over decades.

My advice would be to see the parents you are about to meet – or the ones you have already formed a new social group with through your antenatal classes – as additional friends who offer different things. You don't have to stay best mates with each other forever, but at a time when you are all going through something new and scary, it can be really great to have a network of other people doing the same. Even if you feel like you don't need them, they might need you. So, give it a go. What's the worst that could happen? Answer: you end up friends with an estate agent. But if you really want to get out of a new friendship, you can always move or fake your own death.

New parent friends will be great companions on your new child-based activities too. But most importantly, they are your quickest route back to the pub. Your partner probably isn't too keen on your suggestion that you go out for a regular day session with the lads. But meeting up with one of the other parents from that couple who seemed lovely from the baby dancing class seems a much more responsible and respectable way to go to the very same pub at the very same time and have the very same amount of pints.

JEN BRISTER: To be honest, I struggled when they were babies. I could never make friends at mother and baby groups, probably because I was always overwhelmed with having two babies to look after. But also, because I didn't have the energy or inclination to talk about the weather, I'd find myself being too honest: 'My son did a shit so huge it went up his entire back and covered his shoulders. I was actually impressed.' No one needs or wants to hear that.

Also, when you're a new parent there is nothing else going on in your life other than being a parent, so you're dull. I know when my kids were small I had two main topics of conversation: how tired I was and how much sleep other people were getting – 'What do you think you get a night? Eight hours? Cos I'm on three. Just want to know what eight hours feels like. I bet it's lovely. Is it lovely?'

I suppose when my boys were really small the conversations I wanted from other parents was an admission of just how horrific it could be and, if you weren't going to join me in some heavy-duty catharsis, I wasn't interested.

YOUR OLD MATES

The way you socialize has to change when you become a dad and it can affect your current friendships. Some mates will understandably not always want to rearrange their big night out on the town to a park at midday to accommodate your baby, so there will be a bit of readjusting. Unfortunately, you will probably see a few friends a bit less in the near future.

At times, it can make you feel a bit abandoned, like they are still living their fun, responsibility-free lives and they have forgotten about you. But it's quite likely they will be feeling something similar, like you've moved on and left them behind. So, give it a bit of time for everyone to adjust. Your lives might suddenly feel quite far apart, but they will get closer again.

Ideally, you will have some old mates who are having kids at a similar time to you. This can bring you closer together and you can actually spend more time with each other because taking the kids with you legitimizes your boys' days out.

THE GRANDPARENTS

When you reached the age where you could finally move out of your parents' house, you probably thought, 'I love those guys, but I am so glad I don't have to deal with their shit anymore.' Equally, your parents probably thought, 'We love that guy, but thank Christ we don't have to deal with his shit anymore...and we can finally have loud sex again, woohoo!' (Sorry if I've just made you throw up.)

But when you have a baby, they (and all of the other family members you managed to get a comfortable distance from) will come back into your life in a big way. There's a new cuddly person they want to spend time with, so inevitably you'll find yourself spending much more time with them again too. It can be nice to reconnect with your family and see them show such love for your kid. But it can also bring back all of the feelings you had about your family from when you were younger – both good and bad. You might be reminded of how caring one of them is, how domineering one of them is and what an irresponsible halfwit another is. And while you are feeling the pressure to be more grown-up than you have ever been, you might simultaneously be being treated like (and maybe acting like) a kid again.

Even when the relationship is brilliant with your family and you have none of the feelings above, you still have the problem of the time commitment. You have your side of the family and your partner's. Then, there may have been several separations and new marriages. So, all free time can be spent hosting people.

Don't stress about trying to see everyone as much as they'd like because it's impossible. Just do the maths. Work out the amount of time you have free after you take away sleeping, eating, feeding, cleaning up, bathing, working, going to the toilet. Even if that's an entire weekend (it won't be), you have to divide that up between all of the family members (who will all probably think that once a week isn't too much to ask) and that's your entire week full, with no time to see mates or just relax. But don't worry, after the early excitement dies down, you'll find a groove with it all and family will actually help you to get *more* free time as opposed to taking it away. They will hopefully start to offer to mind your child or do some of the other stuff to relieve the stress, like chores.

There will inevitably be competition between grandparents – they will all want to know how much the others are seeing your baby and make sure that they see them slightly more. In the early days, try not to worry about upsetting or offending them. They will be fine. Being a grandparent is the sweetest deal there is. You get all of the good bits (walks in the park, doling out Werther's Originals), but as soon as you've had enough, you can make the excuse that you have to go because you are tired or you need to have your tea at 3pm or whatever. I know that when I'm feeling like I'm not doing very well at being a dad, I can find myself thinking, 'When I become a grandad, that's when I'll come into my own. Just need to get through the next 30 years without damaging my children so much that they refuse to let me be a part of their kids' lives, then it's plain sailing, baby.'

Of course, not everyone has a close support network and some people have family that live much too far away to visit regularly or at all. Even though you have the benefit of not having to constantly host them and regress to your childhood behaviours, it can feel lonely and like you aren't getting any help from anyone. In this instance, don't be afraid to call on friends to help out, even if it's just picking up some shopping for you or asking them to call round for a cup of tea. You might feel reluctant to ask, but people love being able to help out in these really simple ways. Always reach out when you need a hand.

Grandparents' roles

There's no need to decide on exactly what each grandparent's role will be straight away. It will happen naturally and gradually. Some will be full-on at the start, but lose interest. Others will grow closer to your kids as they get older. Some will end up being your childminder. It will all be influenced by how their relationship develops with your kid as well as where they live and how much they offer to help. But when they do offer, take it. Unless you think they are dangerously inept. And, even then, it might be worth the risk for a night off.

It's quite normal that you (or, more likely, your partner) won't feel comfortable leaving your child with someone straight away. Or she might only want to leave the baby with her own mum at first. This isn't a slight on your family. Well, it might be. I don't know what she thinks of your family. But it's also an entirely understandable anxiety from someone who has just been given the responsibility to care for the most precious thing in existence. She knows that she can tell her mum exactly what to do without fear of offending her.

It will calm down, though, and within a few months, you'll be so desperate for sleep, you'll palm them off on the milkman if you get the opportunity.

What do you call your parents and in-laws?

To their faces, I mean. If it wasn't stressful enough to pick a name for your kid, you now have to pick them for several much older people who already have names and have a very strong opinion on what their new one will be.

It's pretty easy with the blokes. The chances are, they will all be 'Grandad'. But with the women, it's a bit more complicated because there are options, so it's handy if they want different ones. It's very easy for this to become quite a big deal at the time, but my advice to you is just to let everyone choose the name that they want because it won't matter in the long run. Your kid is just going to call them whatever they want to call them and that will be the name that sticks. If your mother-in-law wants to be called 'Glamorous Nan' and your baby starts calling her 'Gumbo', her name will be Gumbo.

Opinions

I'm afraid that the way you dad is something that everybody is going to have an opinion on. Most won't voice it (friends, people in the street), but family probably will. Especially parents, grandparents and in-laws.

You are still your parents' child, so they might feel that they can tell you how to look after your new child. Unless you've asked for their opinion, do not listen. The more you listen, the more you will go back and worry about the damage caused by the things in your childhood. It's likely decades since they were doing what you're doing, and parenting, science and health and safety have moved on a lot.

It's hard not to let their opinions change the way that you

operate, though, especially early on when you don't really know what you're doing. You might suspect they think you are being too soft with your kids for instance, then act more sternly. But doing this just isn't fair on your child, who will wonder why you are being inconsistent and get confused. It isn't fair on you either because you shouldn't need to second-guess yourself or feel like you're not doing it right. You've got enough on your plate, dealing with this screaming kid. It might even be unfair on the person you are assuming has this opinion. You don't know what they're thinking, and who gives a fuck anyway. The best thing to do is block the opinions out. It's just you and your child and you should behave with them exactly the way you'd behave with them at home if others weren't observing you. Or, because it's quite difficult to completely block them out, defer the things that you are feeling to later. Tell yourself, 'I don't care what they think right now; they can judge me by my results years from now when my kid is either an MBE or a criminal.' And, by that time, you will have already come to terms with how your parenting approach worked by your Buckingham Palace–prison visit ratio.

Some opinions don't stop with behaviour and I've heard stories of families voicing their opinions about everything, from how much you see them to how much you see other people to how much you work, how much you go out, how much you drink, how much you spend and even how much you're on social media. Some of these sound quite extreme and hopefully don't happen to you, but the general rule with all these opinions is: take them with a pinch of salt. Unless their kid is Barack Obama, they didn't get everything right and if you followed everyone's advice you'd be the worst, most inconsistent dad in the world.

And bear in mind, it is way worse for the mum. It's a lot easier for you to brush off your grandma telling you that you are holding the baby wrong. But if Grandma says that to your partner, it will feel like she's saying she's failing at being a mum. So make sure you've always got your partner's back.

MILESTONES: WHAT TO EXPECT AND WHEN

As you will hear a thousand times, every baby is different, so here is a very rough idea of when your baby might start doing certain things, but try not to worry if they don't meet these milestones exactly as listed – they could reach them weeks or even months later than some of the estimates and it's still not considered unusual.

Weeks 6–8	They give you their first smile.
Week 8	Their neck is strengthening, so they can lift their head 45 degrees.
Week 12	They discover their hands! They will realize that their fingers are all separate and like to have lots of objects with different textures to play with.
Week 13	They start chuckling and babbling and you'll swear you heard them say 'banana' or 'Doncaster', but they didn't.
Week 15	They roll over.

Week 17	Their babbling develops a bit more as they like to mimic the sounds you make. So watch your language.
Months 6–8	They start crawling.
Months 6–9	They sit up.
Months 8–10	They wave.
Months 6–18	They gradually start walking and talking.
Years 31–38	They beat you in an arm wrestle.

I realize how incredibly vague some of this is, but it varies so much across children. There are hundreds of other amazing developments in the first year alone, so try not to focus too much on hitting the next milestone, then the next.

It's also worth noting that for every dad who is celebrating his child hitting a milestone, there will be another dad who's feeling like a failure because his child hasn't. For every child ahead of the average, there has to be a child behind. We experienced this with both of our children and it can feel crap.

But children progress at different rates depending on hundreds of factors. You'll get babies who do little more than slugs for the first 12 months and then start chatting and running within weeks. Equally, I've got a friend whose parents swear he was the most advanced baby anyone had ever seen and now he spends all of his money on conspiracy theory books and ninja stars. So, try not to see milestones as goals to be scored, but as really rough measures for medical professionals to see how your kid is doing at this very early stage. And, if they are concerned at any point, they will let you know and discuss with you how to help your child along.

WHEN YOUR BABY IS SICK

Now you have a baby, you'll have a lot more interaction with health professionals than you ever have before, but don't worry, generally they're always happy to see you because the main focus is your baby, and your baby is cute. There are regular reviews of your baby's health and development at 6–8 weeks, 9–12 months and 2–2.5 years, but you will end up seeing them a lot more than that for advice and to allay your worries. One of the most common interactions we had early on was when we'd go to them with a concern that they probably thought was trivial and were told, 'Well, you know your own baby', which is a bit annoying, because you don't really know your baby that well because you only met them a few weeks ago. You probably know the Domino's delivery bloke better than your baby and you would not be confident assessing whether his belly is more mottled than usual.

I found it made more sense when I worked out that this phrase roughly translates to 'Fuck knows'. From then on, I did a quick translation in my head every time one of them said it to me:

'Do you know why my baby has a red face in the mornings?'
'Fuck knows.'

It's somehow a lot more reassuring, because it doesn't shift the pressure on to the parents and it makes me realize that none of us really have a clue about anything.

Colds

Your first cold must be such an odd and confusing experience as a baby. Imagine it. You've been alive for a few months and everything is going smoothly, people are always nice to you, you've found an excellent food source which happens to be attached to your mum and is also shaped like a pillow. Life. Is. Sweet. Then you suddenly feel terrible and something starts blocking up your head, from the inside. Your airways are slowly getting more and more clogged and you have no idea what the end point to this is. Does your head eventually fill with whatever is blocking it? Does it swell up and pop?

You keep sneezing, which, again, if you've never done it before will feel like your face is exploding. Then stuff starts leaking out of your nose. And it's green. YOUR HEAD IS LEAKING GREEN STUFF. What the fuck?!

You can't communicate any of this to anyone. So, you have no idea what is happening and don't know if your dad realizes how serious this is because he's barely taking any notice. He just looks like he's trying to avoid getting too close to you.

It's no wonder that a baby's mood will be a bit all over the place during this time. Just comfort them as much as you can and help them do the things they can't. For instance, babies can't blow their own noses, so snot will stay stuck there, unless you get involved and help them out. How do you do that? Well, there are a few techniques…

I've heard stories of parents using their own mouths to suck the snot from their kid's nose. If you want to do that, be my guest (you animal). But other, less disgusting options include using a nasal aspirator, which is a little handheld pump that gently sucks your baby's nostril when you squeeze it. This is very satisfying, but can eat up hours of your afternoon. You can step things up with a battery-powered aspirator, which acts like a little snot hoover. Even more satisfying and way easier. Or you can try saline solution – it comes in little squirty bottles you put up the baby's nose and the salt water loosens up the snot. Have some tissues at the ready.

There are even more extreme methods out there too. If you want to see something disgusting and amazing, search online for a video called 'Nasal Irrigation'. In the video, a woman syringes salt water up one of her daughter's nostrils and it floods out of the other, along with an ungodly amount of snot. Afterwards, the baby looks delighted. She does this several times, flushes out a load of snot and eventually the route is clear. It looks so satisfying I wanted to have a go, so I had a look at how to do it at home. I found an explanation of the method and it seemed pretty simple, but at the end it warned: 'Don't use tap water because you risk giving your child a brain-eating amoeba', so I decided to leave it. My baby might need its brain at some point.

Other illnesses

You'll notice that babies can get all sorts of other illnesses that adults don't get and have names that make them sound like something from Victorian times: slapped cheek; hand, foot and mouth; chickenpox; scarlet fever. Both constipation and diarrhoea are common in babies too (sorry). The NHS website gives great detailed descriptions of all of these and more, and we found that the usual advice with baby illnesses is to simply wait it out. But you should always get anything you are worried about checked out because there is no good reason not to. In the time you'd spend fretting about it, you can just phone 111 and get reassurance that all is well. The main things we're always told to watch out for are the signs of meningitis or pneumonia. For meningitis, they are: blotchy skin, getting paler or turning blue; cold hands and feet; a stiff body with jerky movements or else floppy; vomiting; unusual grunting sounds; pain from muscle aches or joints; a rash that doesn't fade when a glass is rolled over it (and I can't tell you how many times you'll do this as a parent). For pneumonia, signs include: a fever; loss of appetite; tiredness; vomiting; diarrhoea; coughing that is painful and produces mucus. If your child shows these symptoms, phone 111 or 999 immediately.

111 calls and doctor visits

If it's an emergency, call 999. But 111 is the number to call if you're not sure how serious it is, which happens a lot. And you should always call if in doubt, even if you feel silly. Better to feel a bit silly and be safe. I suspect 90 per cent of the calls they receive are from worried new parents just like you, so they are always really friendly and helpful.

No matter what you call about, whether it's a fever, a rash or your baby just seems out of sorts, weirdly they always ask you if the child is bleeding from the head. And, more weirdly, you will always glance over to check. After you've answered all of the questions, more often than not they will reassure that you everything is fine, but still send you to the doctor for them to double-check.

Like many people, I try to avoid a trip to the doctor or hospital unless I can actually see my insides on the outside. But when you have a kid, you've just got to change your mindset and always get stuff checked if you are at all worried. You often get a same-day appointment and they are really pleased to see you when you turn up. I suppose from the doctor's point of view, they are going to be seeing people all day anyway. This way, they get to spend ten minutes with a beautiful little giggly thing as opposed to an old, grey, wrinkly thing who isn't likely to giggle (and, if they do, it's creepy).

More often than not, the doctor will reassure you that everything is fine and send you on your way. The same is true of trips to A&E; there will usually be a lot of worry before you go and while you're waiting, but then most times you will leave feeling so much better.

Illnesses and emergencies can be a hard thing to deal with if you find yourself away from your family, as parents sometimes do because of work. I remember being halfway through a run of gigs supporting the fantastic comedian (and contributor to a cracking dad book) Romesh Ranganathan on his tour. We were in Edinburgh and we'd just done a big gig. We got back to the lovely hotel, had a drink in the bar and I almost forgot I was a dad. Then I returned to the room, checked my phone and saw I had a message from my wife to say that she was in hospital with our three-month-old daughter, who was on oxygen. She had been struggling to breathe because she'd developed bronchiolitis.

All I wanted to do was to be with them. I felt selfish for choosing a career that took me away from them and guilty for enjoying myself so much while all this was happening. I was also stuck because all of the trains had stopped and I was 200 miles away.

Luckily, the next night's gig was 25 miles from where the hospital was, so, once I knew my daughter wasn't in danger and I knew that I wouldn't be able to get there much quicker by not doing the gig, we arranged that the next night I'd do my 20 minutes of observations about stick insects or whatever it was I was doing before Romesh came on, then my father-in-law would pick me up from the venue and take me straight to the hospital.

It was one of the strangest nights of my life. I was on stage, telling jokes to the biggest audience I'd ever played to, knowing my daughter was lying in hospital. It completely summed up the contradictions of fatherhood for me. You can feel everything at once, all of the time; the nauseating worry for my daughter, the guilt that I wasn't with her and my wife, the responsibility to work and the thrill of the thing I was actually doing at the time, which added to the guilt.

When I came off stage, I was ushered by one of the venue staff all the way to the stage door where my father-in-law was waiting for me with the engine running. Ninety-nine per cent of me just wanted to get to the hospital; one per cent of me really enjoyed this rock-star exit from the gig. I was with my wife and daughter within the hour, we stayed in hospital for a few days and my daughter made a full recovery.

As horrible as it is, it's very likely that something like this will happen to you at some point and you probably won't know how to deal with it and it will be awful. But it is par for the course for parents and the good thing is that the overwhelming odds are that everything will be OK.

Immunizations

Your baby will be offered a series of vaccines and immunizations (well, you will on their behalf) to protect them from diseases like meningitis, measles, mumps and rubella. They happen at 8 weeks, 12 weeks, 16 weeks and 1 year. Taking your baby to have their injections is a job that might appeal to you because it's something that feels like it's going to be a quick win, with added points for bravery – exactly the type of tasks dads go for. But it's not a nice one. You are taking your baby to be given something that will hurt them. Even though you know it's for their own good, it won't feel natural.

When I walked in, the nurse greeted me by telling me, 'A lot of mums cry at this, but I've never had a dad cry.' It was as if she was warning me because she could sense I might be the man to ruin her 100 per cent record.

It's only when you get in the room that you realize you're not just there to comfort the baby. No, you are the accomplice. It's your job to pin your kid down while the nurse sticks several needles in them, which look massive next to their little legs. You'll find this emotionally confusing. It will go against every protective instinct in your body. But you have to do it and you have to hold them really tightly because, if they move, which they will try to do, it'll hurt more.

The look they will give you after the first needle is heartbreaking. Even though they are only a few weeks old, they will look at you like you have betrayed their trust. You are supposed to keep them from harm, but you are doing the opposite. You'll want to smile to cheer them up, but then think that will be even more upsetting for them. What type of sicko smiles at you while they are pinning you down for someone to stick needles in you?! So you'll probably settle on a look that says, 'I know, I'm sorry.'

Rest assured, this won't be as traumatizing for your baby as it seems. You won't believe how quickly they get over it. In our case, as soon as it was done, the nurses shook some loud musical instruments at my kid and he instantly forgot what had happened, while I was about to break the nurse's no-crying record.

Babies can get a little bit ill after injections, but it's rarely anything too serious. Just a bit of a sore leg, a fever and maybe a sleepless night. But you'll be awake anyway, with PTSD.

DAD TRICK One thing I often do when I'm feeling really sorry for my baby is recontextualize it. They are cute and helpless now, but that won't last long. One day, they will be a 40-year-old who doesn't visit you enough in your old age and only ever buys you socks for your birthday. Imagine the person they will become and it makes it a lot easier to handle.

Anti-vaxxers

Some people won't let their kids have vaccines because they think it will do more harm than good. Some suspect it causes things like autism and some simply think it's a way for the government to put microchips in us to control our minds. Everyone has a right to refuse vaccines, but if everyone did, viruses would spread much more quickly and cause more harm to more people, so it is cutting your nose off to spite everyone's face. Though, I suppose I am bound to say that because my mum let them put the government microchip in me.

More serious illnesses

It's every parent's biggest worry. It's what we think about every time we see a rash or hear a cough, and it will be that way for years. There have been hundreds of times when I've felt like this. There have been tens of times where I've driven my kid to A&E and have been sick with worry. And there have been a couple of times when I've spent time on the children's ward and tried to make a deal with a God I don't believe in to take my life if he has to take someone's.

Thankfully – and I am more thankful of this than anything – my kids have always recovered fully from any illness they've had. But, of course, there are children who don't and suffer serious and terminal illnesses. To the parents of these children, I'm so sorry that you have to go through this. It must be the worst pain a person can suffer. All you can do is know that your role as their dad and your love and care is more important now than it will be at any other point in your life and it means everything to your child.

Baby medicine

You will undoubtedly end up with more stuff than this and you'll probably find your own preferences with brands, but these are the essentials we always try to have in. Make sure you check the recommended ages on everything before giving it to your baby.

- **General:** Calpol, ibuprofen for babies (both now come in liquid form with syringes to make it easy to give to your baby), a decent thermometer
- **Wind:** gripe water, Infacol
- **Teething:** Anbesol, teething granules
- **Colds:** saline nose spray, vapour rub or oil (Vicks BabyRub, Olbas oil or Snufflebabe)
- **Nappy rash:** Sudocrem, Metanium (for when it's severe)

When stocking up, you'll notice that a lot of baby products come in packaging that looks like it hasn't changed for 50 years. I see that as a good sign. If your product sells well without any advertising or any attempt to modernize the packaging, it must be pretty decent stuff.

DAD TRICK When giving your child medicine using a syringe, angle it to the inside of their cheek. If you point it directly into their mouth, it will hit the back of their throat, and they will splutter and think you're a wanker.

MORE STUFF, NOW

It will astound you how quickly babies need new clothes. My wife will buy our daughter some leggings from the supermarket when she does the weekly shop and she'll have grown out of them by the time the bag of salad in the veg drawer has started to go brown. Kids grow at an alarming rate and you'll constantly hear the phrase, 'She needs more…' followed by a combination of two numbers, which won't make an awful lot of sense to you: 'She needs more 3–6'; 'She needs more 9–12'. But it basically means: money is about to get spent.

You're probably thinking about how to avoid the cost of this insatiable appetite for new clothes. Well, you've got two options: either quibble over everything and lose every argument anyway because, when you're told 'She needs it', what can you possibly say back to that? 'I'll make her something'? No. Or just bury your head in the sand.

I have no idea what half of the clothes are that a child needs and I have no idea what's a good price for a kid's cardigan, so I just don't get involved and I'm grateful my wife is handling it. If we end up bankrupt, so be it, we'll go and live in a shed with our incredibly stylish children.

Accept hand-me-downs if you are offered them. Kids grow so quickly, the chances are it'll only have been worn a couple of times. If you read this in enough time, try to befriend some rich, trendy people with a kid a few months older than yours.

BEING DAD

This brand-new job is going to bring out different qualities in you. You won't become a completely different person, just the dad version of yourself. You will be more responsible and better at putting up shelves, but you will also inevitably get grumpier and more boring, and will start complaining about the heating being on all the time.

There's no problem in these traits coming out. Like everything we do in life, you have to play different roles in different situations because that's what it's appropriate to do. You wouldn't act the same way at a kid's party as you would on a stag do, although they do have similar levels of vomit.

But the key is to not become 100 per cent dad. We all know those people whose job defines them, who act like an accountant whether they are in the office or on a crazy golf course. I certainly know comedians who are constantly performing whether they are onstage or eating breakfast. These people are more exhausting than kids. So, it's great to act like a dad with your kids, but don't be 'dad' with your partner and your mates because they will start to find you very dull.

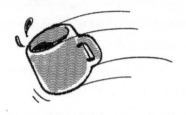

CHAPTER 8

THREE TO SIX MONTHS

By three months old, your little one will have started to develop their own personality and you will have probably forgotten what life was like before they were here. Your baby will be the main thing you talk about (apart from sleep, of course) and one of the main things you think about. But there might be something else that has started to edge its way back into your thoughts recently…

SEX

Yes, you are currently in the biggest dry spell you've had since you bought that leather jacket. But even though you're probably ready to go at the drop of a hat, be patient. You might try to put your 'moves' on her a few times and, when she somehow doesn't bow to your powers of seduction (reaching your arm over in bed and touching her back for 20 seconds), think, 'Right, I'm not trying any more' because you're a sensitive little flower. But there are a lot of reasons why she might be holding off.

For a start, it takes a while to physically recover from birth. The average is around three months, but it can take a year or so for everything to fully return to normal. So there's the worry that sex will be uncomfortable or painful. She might also be feeling unattractive or self-conscious, and she'll definitely be feeling knackered. Any spare minute that isn't spent sleeping might well seem frivolous.

So, try not to put too much pressure on it, but equally let her know how attractive you still find her. Tell her there's no rush, but whenever she's ready, you are. In fact, you probably won't need to say that second bit, she'll be able to tell by the amount of glasses you keep knocking off tables with your permanent erection.

When you do both decide the time is right to go again, don't expect to just pick up where you left off. You might both even feel a bit shy or nervous because it's been so long. Then you feel awkward that you feel shy and nervous. But it's to be expected. When you stop doing it for too long, sex can seem like a very odd thing to do. And, physically, it'll probably feel a bit different at first. She might find it uncomfortable and the sensation might be different for you too. But don't worry, this isn't how it's always going to be. Her body is still readjusting from what happens when you have a baby and, after a few weeks, you'll notice things are slowly returning to how they were.

Don't let a tricky start put you off. The more sex you have, the more you'll both want and the quicker it'll get back to how it was before. It's definitely harder to have a full sex life when you've got a kid. Opportunities are rarer and you are both tired. Your new baby is probably sleeping next to you for the first six months and, if you're anything like me, you'll find it terribly off-putting having a relative in the room.

Your minds are on other things these days as well and your lives are completely different. It's not so easy to quickly switch from disagreements about who has changed the most nappies to dirty talk. If you do find that easy, I don't want you reading my book, you pervert.

But it's good that you both talk about it, even if you are not ready. Eventually, you will be. And when you decide to start having sex again, it will bring you closer. It will remind you that you have a relationship that isn't just a working partnership. And it's probably all you've been thinking about for the last few months, so it will mean you can finally get some other stuff done.

BECOMING LESS SELFISH

Without wanting to sound like a wooden sign in your auntie's kitchen, becoming a parent brings a whole new meaning to your life.

You've probably spent the last few decades thinking about yourself, first and foremost. Not because you're selfish, but because it's natural. Throughout your childhood, your education and your career, your main focus is 'What do I want to do with MY life? What will I become? Who do I want to be?' When your partner came into your life, you will have had to adjust a little bit.

But now there's a baby, you're going to experience the biggest shift of all. You have a new priority that completely wipes out everything else. And you are going to need to offer even more of yourself to support your partner. That's the thing that might be an unexpected readjustment. I think you assume that you'll have to start prioritizing your baby. But you also need to realize that your partner has a brand-new, all-consuming priority too, so she will need more of your help and have a much lower tolerance for your shit.

It's hard to admit that something you've always done is selfish. But that's not necessarily what is happening. Some things which weren't selfish before can become so when you're a parent because the rules have changed. For example, playing five-a-side: probably still fine, but maybe not as regularly. Your best mate's stag do: as long as you're not using the money you need for baby food, you should be OK. But the stag do of that lad who goes in the pub and you're not sure of his real name but everyone calls Slug Man: you'll have to give that one a miss now.

YOUR RELATIONSHIP (AND HOW NOT TO BE A DICKHEAD)

I love to watch sports documentaries. They are the closest I'll ever come to being part of an American football team (because of my other work commitments, physical ability, genetic make-up, age, diet, lack of talent and I don't know the rules), but I also enjoy them because I learn stuff about the different team dynamics and the psychology of very successful sports teams.

The teams I'd most like to be a part of are the ones with a coach who puts an arm around their players when they are having a bad day and builds them up. I wouldn't want to play for a coach who stands on the sidelines yelling about the unfairness of it all every time something doesn't go their way. Although they are definitely the most fun ones to watch.

So, what I've learned to try to do and, I have to admit, I don't always manage it – in fact, if you were to ask my wife, she'd probably be bewildered by this claim – but what I *try* to do is be the person I'd want around the house.

Unless you have other kids, you are a third of the population of your home, so your mood has a huge impact on the overall feeling of this mini society. Your bad mood can put everyone in a bad mood, but on the other side of the coin, you have a lot of power to make things good.

Sometimes if the other person is grumpy and you feel they have no right to be, your instinct will be to think, 'Why are you unhappy? I am the one who got up early/worked today/has a bad back, blah blah blah.' Although a natural reaction, it's petty and it's not going to make things better. It just adds to the amount of pissed-off people in the house. One of the times I love my wife most is when I'm moping about the house in a bad mood and the kids are yelling and, instead of snapping at us all, she brightens everything up with a happy voice and a hug or the offer of a cuppa.

So, a good little trick, although it seems counter-intuitive, is the moment you feel pissed off, do something nice for your family (even if it's them you are pissed off with). Do a little chore that no one else wants to do or get everyone a little treat. The satisfaction of doing a simple task will instantly improve things (worst-case scenario, you're still in a bad mood but now the washing up has been done). But what's likely to happen is your family will be happier, because you've just done something nice for them and you'll be happier, because it feels good to do nice things for the people you love.

Do not mistake this for the passive-aggressive martyrdom people do when they see the hoovering hasn't been done and get so annoyed they do it themselves angrily to prove a point. The attitude behind a move like that is the complete opposite and is likely to just piss everyone off more.

JEN BRISTER: Sometimes you have to give each other a break, because there is no time off when you're a parent to young children. It's all very well saying you should carve out time for yourself, but there are days where it's just not possible. So, if you see your other half doing all the housework, struggling with the baby, trying to prepare dinner...maybe don't bring up how boring your last Zoom meeting was. It's really helpful if you can pre-empt that moment where they pick up your favourite mug and threaten to throw it at your head.

It's so important to have a bit of your day where you're not with your kids. We do try to give each other that time alone. I have been so desperate to be on my own I have taken up sea swimming – I go most mornings. I don't care if it's snowing outside, I'M SWIMMING. Chlo likes to go for a run, or a walk, or just lock herself in a cupboard to hear the sound of her own breathing. When you're stuck in the house with kids, it's a lot harder, which is why I try not to feel guilty about screen time. The highlight of my day might be if I get to drink my coffee while listening to a podcast. That is beyond bliss and if it means sticking Netflix on for an hour, I'm going to bloody well do it.

RUSSELL KANE: If anything, becoming a parent made my relationship with my wife even better. We'd seen how it had gone wrong for other people so we made the decision to double down on 'us'. We make a real effort to do dates, watch movies together and have nights away.

Another unexpected thing that might affect your relationship with your partner is the redirection of affection. I would assume that your partner has been the main focus of your affection until now, unless you are a philanderer or a weird dog person. But now you have a brand-new thing in your life that you will both spend a huge amount of time cuddling and kissing, so it can be easy to stop cuddling and kissing each other without really noticing. With this in mind, a great habit to get into is to just make sure that when you come home and give your kid a kiss and a cuddle, you always give your partner one too. The fact that your relationship might not seem like the priority any more is exactly why you should put even more effort into it.

There's always a score being kept

If you are bringing up this baby as a couple you will have probably planned to work together and both do your fair bit. But neither of you will be able to be completely selfless and you will both be keeping score constantly. If you get up more in the night, change a nappy or do a feed, you'll be sticking points on your own tally. She'll be doing the same with hers. And if either of you feels like it doesn't balance out, resentment will grow.

But it's more complicated than it seems because you'll both have entirely different scoring systems. Things that you are sure will get you a load of points, might not get you anything according to her system. You might even be docked points. And I promise you, you're not aware of half of the points she has been racking up.

One way of dealing with this is to lash out at the whole system and refuse to even acknowledge the points. But that's futile. The game still continues. The points tally never ceases. Also, this sort of behaviour will cost you hundreds.

So, it's a good idea to not make a big deal of the stuff you are doing while quietly accumulating so many points your performance is unignorable. And, once you've established yourself as a consistent point-getter (not a sporting term), you'll come under less scrutiny. This might not seem fair, but it isn't fair that her body has been destroyed by the baby you put there, so I probably wouldn't bring up the subject of fairness if I were you.

I know, blokes need to be told 'Well done' for every single chore they do. But if you can delay your gratification slightly, this technique implies you've done more and will get you more praise in the long term. If you let her discover some of your work for herself, she will be thinking, 'Wow, if he's folded all the clothes without even mentioning it, he's probably done loads of other things I don't know about too', instead of 'All he's done this week is taken the bins out and I know that because he announced it three times.'

But points aren't *really* the aim, because you can never win that game. What you actually want to focus on is making your partner feel good because you love them. A really important thing to do is to acknowledge all of her struggles and work. You know how much you need to air all of the crap you've dealt with today? Well, she needs that too. So, instead of always telling her how much you've done first, thank her for the things she's done. Ask how her night's sleep was. Ask her if she needs you to do anything for her today. Offer to give her a bit of time to herself because she's had the kids all day. And do this even when you think you've done a load too. Even when you think you've had a tougher day.

The added bonus is the more you do this, the more she'll do it back. And that's when it becomes a happy household where you both feel appreciated. And once you've achieved this harmony, that's when you float the idea of going away on Smithy's stag do to Ibiza.

Separation

As much as you both might try to help each other and do the best for your relationship and your family, having a kid puts all sorts of new strains on a relationship and it's an unfortunate truth that it can get too much and couples sometimes split up. It's probably not what you had planned and it will be an incredibly difficult thing to go through. You'll have to reimagine your whole future, you'll worry about the effect it will have on your child and you'll have to do this while dealing with all of the usual heartbreak a person has when a relationship ends. There's no denying it will be a tough part of your life, but a lot of people have to go through it and it doesn't need to negatively affect your child in the long term. My parents split up when I was very young, the same happened with my wife's parents, and plenty of the best people I know have parents who separated. The thing is, not everyone can stay in love forever and not every relationship can last a lifetime. It's much better for a child to have two happier separated parents than ones who are staying together unhappily. If you find yourself going through a break-up, you just need to find a new way to make it work as co-parents, which you will manage to do, although it does have its challenges, as my friend Ivo Graham describes:

IVO GRAHAM: I suppose one upside to co-parenting is that you have something vaguely leftfield to contribute to your friend George's book. I'd have to say, sadly, that really is the only upside to it, so if you're reading this as a current/prospective co-parent and you don't EVEN have a friend compiling a book about parenting, well, I've got to say: gutted for you and your lack of outlet!

All flippancy aside – and flippancy isn't the healthiest of all the coping mechanisms, but it serves me well enough – I have adored so many aspects of new parenthood, even when going through it in the trenches of a break-up. The joys of watching my daughter start to take shape – laughing, crawling, walking, talking, dabbing, flossing – have been by some distance the most moving moments of my life (and I've watched Arcade Fire on MDMA). And for all the myriad stresses, regrets and synced iCals of doing that outside a 'traditional' family unit, I've been pleasantly surprised (slash, heartbreakingly relieved) by how little those complications have punctured through to the emotional core of the journey. My ex and I still get to share aspects of that journey together, while knowing that, however tough it is doing it this way, our futures, and our daughter's, will be all the happier for it.

Or maybe not! It's early days. It might completely destroy us! Do try to have a child with the right person if at all possible. Otherwise, come join me in Silver Liningsville. Time to get some of that sleep back!

FAVOURITISM

We all like some people more than others. Of course we do. But politeness and awareness of people's feelings usually stops us from making it too obvious. Children don't have these concerns. They will make it quite clear who they like most and, when it comes to the parents, that can cause issues. The person who they like least feels hurt and the one they like most has to constantly play with them, pick them up, feed them, put them to bed, while telling the other one, 'They do love you, they are just going through a stage' or 'Hahahaha, I'm the best', depending on how much of a prick you are.

When this clear favouritism is going on, you have to try to focus on the positives, and there are positives on both sides. The one they didn't pick, who we'll call the 'The Loser', at least has their freedom and can watch TV in peace without a baby clambering over their face. The one in favour, 'The Winner', has the comfort of knowing they are the best parent.

But don't celebrate or commiserate too much because, like most things with kids that seem like big issues at the time, it will soon change. Babies and toddlers are fickle little people and they can flip in a heartbeat. I remember when I was top dog. Constantly showered with love, I was king of the world, obviously feeling bad for my wife, but ultimately, loving it. It felt like the good times were never going to end.

Then something changed. He became distant. He no longer looked at me in the same way. I sat him down and asked him outright, 'There's someone else isn't there? Tell me! If you have any respect left for me at all, tell me who she is.' But he didn't have the vocabulary or the balls to give me a straight answer.

My wife was suddenly the one he preferred. But it was way more extreme than it had been with me. When I was the main man, we just noticed a slight preference. But with her, the love was all-consuming, and it manifested in a dislike for me. The thought that I would replace his beloved mum in any of the key situations (bedtime, watching cartoons, nursery drop off) brought about in him a rage like I've not seen since Ken Barlow had a fight with Mike Baldwin over Deirdre in the middle of the street. I had become a threat to their relationship.

All you can do when you find yourself in this situation is to try not to take it too personally and know that it will pass. Or have another kid and make them *your* favourite. But what you're more likely to do, if you're anything like me, is sulk because no one likes you and watch reruns of old episodes of *Coronation Street* for comfort.

ELIS JAMES: I think I spend more time with them than the average dad, and this is all to do with the flexibility of my job, so I consider myself very lucky. Having comedians as parents means that only one thing matters, and over fish fingers, beans and waffles yesterday our daughter confirmed that I am 'the funniest one'. That said, if I try to give Isy a hug in the kitchen, our son will push me away and shout 'NO,' so I think it's currently 1–1.

ROMESH RANGANATHAN: Because of work hours I don't often do bedtimes. One night, Leesa had gone out, and I assured her that I would have no problems at all with putting the kids to bed. I don't know if the three of them had collaborated to come up with a plan, but they all started telling me they didn't see me enough and it would be nice to hang out and do dad and son stuff. If it had been a cartoon my head would have been replaced by a donkey as I let them stay up later to do family things, under the pretence of wanting to hang out with their dad. My wife came home, and I explained to her that the boys had just really wanted to hang out and that we had a magical evening. She didn't have the heart to tell me then, but a few days later she explained that I had just been victim of a father–son mugging off.

CHILDCARE

When to put your kid in childcare, like just about everything else to do with parenting, is the subject of much debate. Some believe it's damaging to put them in childcare too early, while some believe it's damaging to keep them at home for too long. But take the fact that there are such opposing views as reassurance that, whatever you choose to do – or are forced to do out of circumstance – a huge proportion of parents will passionately feel that you are doing the right thing. And, don't worry, there are lots of benefits to doing it both ways. So, let's forget about whether you should or shouldn't, because that conversation could last forever. And let's talk more about when you can do it and what the options are.

You can put your kid into childcare from a surprisingly early age, with a lot of nurseries offering care from three months and a few offering it even earlier. The same goes for childminders.

It can be expensive, though, and if your wages don't cover the costs early on, it might make sense to wait until the government schemes kick in to help with the cost. Tax breaks for working parents and free hours for those on Universal Credit start earlier, but the most widely used help – the '15/30 free hours' initiative – comes into play the school term after the child's third birthday. This is also when a lot of pre-school nurseries start taking children (these are a good transition to proper school).

But many parents still opt to keep their kid at home or use other childcare until school age and, like I say, there is no right or wrong…unless you go on the Mumsnet forums, then you will learn that everything is both right and wrong at the same time.

Who?
When you eventually need a hand, there are a few different options. Most people won't have all available to them, but let's discuss the possibilities.

Grandparents
When your parents or in-laws (or other family members, for that matter) look after your child, it's comforting, because you know they will really care for them and it's lovely for kids to be close to grandparents. To your kid, grandparents probably feel like the nearest thing to you that isn't you. But of all the childcare options, they are likely to be the least au fait with the latest techniques (see page 170). The other drawback is that it gives your child the least amount of bonding with kids of their

own age. Because their main interaction will be with someone who's half a century older than them, they might pick up some unusual habits, like watching the snooker or drinking sherry in the afternoon.

Nannies

I know these will be financially unattainable for most people, but the benefits are, of course, the flexibility, the ease, the total dedication to your child and the chance that they just might be magic and take your kid on musical adventures across the rooftops of London.

Childminders

This is the halfway point between family and nursery. There are usually a few other kids at a childminder's, but not loads. And they are normally a bit cheaper than nursery, but more expensive than family. They will give you a personal approach, but it's not as personal as Grandma, so your kid won't hear stuff like, 'You're fascinated with your testicles, just like your father was.' The key with a childminder is finding one you absolutely love because they will become a huge part of your child's life and the single person who they spend most time with apart from you, unlike at nursery, where the care is shared by several different people.

ELIS JAMES: Childminders are, in my experience, more imaginative when it comes to activities for the children, and it socializes the kids and allows them to make friends. Our kids go to a childminder rather than a nursery, and she feels more like part of the family.

Nursery

A lot of parents worry that their child won't get as much personal attention in a nursery compared to the other options. I suppose it really depends on the nursery, but a good one will feel personal and there will generally be a great mix of interaction with both adults and children of a similar age. It's a really nice feeling to know that, when you leave your kid at nursery, you're leaving them with people whose vocation it is to look after children like yours. They seem like really fun places for kids because they are kitted out with lots of stuff to keep them entertained, and the food is often fantastic because many of them have a kitchen to prepare varied and well-balanced meals.

As you've probably guessed, it's usually the most expensive option, apart from a nanny. But it's always worth checking the financial help available to you because you might be surprised by how much you can get.

In the end, we decided to send our first child to nursery. But once you've made that decision, you have to find one…

Choosing a nursery

You probably won't know what you want from a nursery until you start visiting them and see what you don't want. So, get out there and visit as many as you can, ideally within walking distance of your house or on your way to work (because you'll be back and forth a lot). You'll soon get a feel for the type of place you'd be happy to leave your kid for the day. When we were looking, I went to our two closest nurseries and they both gave me completely different impressions.

The first one I went to just didn't feel right, and it was mainly because of the way the staff were standing – outside the door with fags in their mouths. I'm not against people who smoke, but I also don't want my kid to come home with a twenty-a-day habit. I've got enough outgoings these days without paying for a baby's Benson & Hedges. But the next nursery we went to gave me a much nicer feeling. The woman who greeted me at the door was like someone from children's TV; exactly the type of person I imagined I would leave my child with. Who knows, maybe she's got a crack habit behind closed doors, but she kept it well hidden and that was good enough for me. The nursery instantly felt like a place I'd be happy to leave my kid. But thinking it and doing it are two very different things…

Leaving your kid at nursery

Most nurseries will ease your child (and you) in with a few taster sessions where you stay and play for a while together. But inevitably the moment will come when you have to walk away, leaving your child there and they will look at you like you are abandoning them and might never come back. The cruelty you feel when you first do this is probably even more than you'd expect. At the nursery we went to, they encouraged me to leave, but said I could stay in the parents' room for 15 minutes if it would really make me feel better. That way, I'd know they could get me if they needed me. I did this, and it did not make me feel better. I just sat there listening to my son crying his eyes out because he didn't know where I was and where he was. It felt like one of those unethical thought experiments from the sixties you will have learned about if you did AS-level Psychology.

The nursery staff will be keen to get you out as quickly as

possible because the process is always the same: the kid will get very upset and then…they are fine. Generally, this will happen quicker if you leave earlier so, as unnatural as it will feel, the kindest thing to do for your kid, yourself and definitely for the nursery staff is to leave as soon as they tell you to. If you picked a nursery that feels right and you like the staff, then trust them. They do this all the time.

Something else that happens is you really appreciate and look forward to the time to yourself, and you shouldn't feel guilty about that. As much as you love spending time with your child, you realize how important it is for your head to have time when you're not worrying about them. And because you appreciate this time so much more, you'll likely use it for something more productive like work, or sleep, or FIFA Career Mode.

DAD TRICK The three techniques I use to help in a situation like this are as follows:

1. Give it a bit of distance. Imagine looking back on this in a few years. It really won't be a big deal then. No kid is traumatized by the first time they were left at nursery.

2. Ask yourself what the alternative is. Never leave your kid anywhere? They will end up being that weird guy at university.

3. Imagine that it's somebody else's kid. This never fails to give you a bit of perspective. Pretend you are an onlooker and it's either one of your friend's children or just a stranger's. You'd probably think to yourself, 'Well,

yes, of course the kid is crying, but it's not the end of the world and you're making it worse by hanging around and getting stressed out. Just go and have a coffee and forget about it, mate.'

JOSH WIDDICOMBE: Would it be terrible to say I felt elated the first time we left our daughter at nursery? Obviously, you are meant to worry about her, but she was in the hands of the professionals; if we can get away with keeping her happy and alive, then they aren't going to have a problem. I feel forever indebted to the people who look after her at nursery, like you would to someone who has saved your life. I would like to think this is because I feel I owe them so much for bringing happiness and security into my daughter's life even when we are not there, but I worry it is because their work allows me to have breakfast on my own in the café round the corner.

If you don't like it, change it

It's worth bearing in mind if you ever get to the point where you don't feel comfortable about the experience your kid is having, you always have the option to change nursery, nanny or childminder, although it is a *little* trickier to change grandparents. You need to feel confident at all times that you've left your kid in the care that feels right. I've heard anecdotes of a child's key worker changing and the child stopping enjoying nursery. Or parents getting the feeling that some of the staff there don't really like their child. If you feel like this, you can ask for a meeting with them. If nothing gets better, it's easy enough to find something new. There are always options.

Nursery bugs

When you first go into your child's nursery, you can't help but notice all of the snot. Every kid has green gunk coming from their nose and they always gravitate towards an adult when they walk into the room. When they are close, they're like the dogs at the park with slobber around their mouths and you're worried one of them will get it on your jeans. The best thing to do is remain entirely still and hope they don't notice you.

It's no wonder there is so much snot everywhere when you survey the scene for more than a minute. It's boiling hot in there – so the perfect Petri dish for germs – and these little people put everything in their mouths: toys, each other's dummies, each other's hands. So, it shouldn't be a surprise that for the first few weeks of nursery your kid will be constantly snotty, disgusting and sick, and so will you. (For tips on this refer to the illnesses section on page 174.) But the good news is, it will build up both your immune systems. So, get that first couple of months of constant runny noses out of the way and your family will become indestructible. If we're ever in a chemical war, you will survive and be rulers of the world.

YOU'RE NOT COOL ANYMORE

You've seen the other dads out and about with their walking boots and their fleeces and you've probably thought, 'That will never, ever be me. I'm going to stay young and relevant, and everyone I speak to will not believe that someone as cool as me could possibly be a dad.'

But we all thought that, mate. And, I'm sorry, but it gets you. It won't happen instantly and for those first few months you'll feel like you managed to hang on to your old image. But the gradual shift has started without you even realizing it. It happens over hundreds of tiny decisions. You'll start picking practicality over style, just listening to music that you know is good instead of wasting time trying to find something new. All of these choices make complete sense in isolation, but each is a small step towards the moment you wake up and put on your fleece and walking boots.

Even though the thought of becoming incredibly uncool might sound horrifying to you now, in practice, it's quite liberating. You can embrace the dad bod because it is expected of you now. You can stop trying to stay up to date with fashion. And there's just no denying that fleeces are comfy.

Another positive is that you'll start to notice that the bar has suddenly become a lot lower. No one is expecting a dad to be cool or sexy, so you get double points for the things that you do. You might not have been anything to write home about when you were a bachelor, but now you're in a new category and it's one with much lower quality competition. With a lot less effort, you can become cool or even, dare I say it, a DILF. You'll probably have to lose the walking boots for that though.

CHAPTER 9

SIX TO TWELVE MONTHS

Six months in and you'll be getting used to the fact that you can never really get used to anything when it comes to babies. Their rate of development over this time is crazy and every day seems to bring with it a new challenge you need to overcome. Even though there are lots of complicated and difficult things to deal with that make you think, 'Oh, bloody hell, what now…?', you'll also notice there are more and more things your child does that make you fall further in love with them. It's hard to describe how wonderful, fulfilled and utterly in love your child can make you feel with the simplest of looks or noises. I know because I tried and then deleted it out of embarrassment. But it's around this time that they will start teething, which is probably more in the camp of 'Oh, bloody hell, what now…?'

IT'S ALWAYS TEETHING

Babies start growing their first set of teeth at around six months, but it can be a lot later (up to around twelve months) and, indeed, a lot earlier (some babies are actually born with teeth!), but whenever it comes, you can almost guarantee that this will be the number-one cause of your baby's problems. Not only does it cause constant dribbling (that's where those muslins and bibs really come into their own), but many parents report it correlates with fevers, rashes, messy nappies, sore bums, very bad moods and general illness. On the one hand, it's really distressing that this one inevitable development all babies have to go through will cause your child so many problems. On the other hand, it's nice, as the beginner parent, to have one ailment that will explain almost everything.

DAD TRICK The perfect phrase for the learner dad whenever there's a problem is: 'Might be teething…'; more often than not, you'll be right. I don't think I'll ever stop using it. When my daughter arrives home in tears at 23 years old and says, 'I'm leaving him, he's such a bastard!', I'll undoubtedly turn to my wife and say, 'Don't worry, she's probably just teething.'

You can understand why it is such a problem-causer. Remember how upset your baby got the last time they dropped their comforter? Well, now they are going to experience the feeling of a sharp piece of enamel slowly being pushed through the flesh in their head over the course of a few weeks. So, you can imagine, emotions will run high.

We've found that the best way to combat it is with a combination of Calpol and Anbesol. Anbesol is an over-the-counter numbing antiseptic and anaesthetic you rub on the gums and Calpol is a delicious magic potion that contains paracetamol, but tastes like strawberries made out of sugar. Anbesol comes in a tiny bottle, which I've always thought implies strength. And I can vouch for its effectiveness. I now use it on the ulcers I get when I'm run down because I've been up all night with a teething baby. Be careful when applying it on your baby's gums, though – when a baby has a finger shoved in their mouth, they are likely to clamp down, so use the finger you'd be least upset to lose.

In fact, like a puppy, your baby will chew on everything.

Clothes, slippers, books. You can buy special plastic and rubber chewing things for this purpose. But, as with toys you've bought for them and want them to play with, babies can sense your desperation. If you've spent a tenner on a chewable monkey and you really, really want your baby to use it, sorry pal, they will use your phone case instead.

It's not always teething

The most upset my daughter ever got as a baby was on Christmas Eve. She just would not stop crying for hours and hours. And, as usual, we said, 'She's teething.' Eventually, she cried herself to sleep at about 2am. On Christmas Day, we were tired and at the end of our tethers when our son started crying his eyes out too. But he was upset for a different reason. He was struggling to complete a jigsaw, because some of the pieces were half eaten. We realized who had been feeding on the jigsaw when we changed our daughter's nappy and found the metaphorical and actual missing piece to the puzzle. We looked at it and felt relieved, she looked at it and looked relieved, our son looked at it and was more distressed than ever.

Brushing teeth

From my personal focus group of two, it seems children will either immediately love or hate brushing their teeth. If they love it, great. Take the rest of this section off. If they don't, you've got work to do.

The recommended advice is for you to brush your kid's teeth yourself until they are three years old, although you can understand why this might not be enjoyable for the kid. Try to imagine how it must feel to have someone brush your teeth for you without gagging.

So, you'll need to do a few other things to try to make them see brushing their teeth as a positive experience. You can do it in the bath, in front of a mirror, while singing a song or while doing something else fun at the same time. Give different toothbrushes and flavours of toothpaste a go too. Even if it takes a little while, like with most bits of parenting, investing the time early can save you much more in the long run and they will soon get used to the routine.

WEANING

Weaning is the process of introducing your baby to solid foods and starts when they're about six months old, because at this point they need more than just milk to meet their needs. It's yet another sign your baby is becoming more like a human and less like a hedgehog.

Before you start, you need to make sure your baby is at the point where they can stay in a sitting position and hold their head steady, as well as coordinate their eyes, hands and mouth (so they can put food in and take food out of their mouth). If they can't do these things, they are not quite ready and you should wait a few more weeks.

Ideally, you took my earlier advice and booked a new parents' first aid course before you got to this point, or at least have watched a few videos on what to do if your child chokes. If you didn't, do it before you start weaning (see page 27).

Because, even though it's unlikely they will choke (they have an inbuilt gag reflex that will instinctively kick in), it will be constantly on your mind and it's such a reassurance if you know what to do.

Your baby has never chewed or swallowed anything solid, so inevitably they are going to be terrible at it when they first try. There will be loads of coughing and spluttering and catching of breath. But the thing that most stuck with me from the first aid course we did was that when you hear that coughing and spluttering (the traditional 'choking' sounds), it is actually a good thing because it means the airways have air coming through and your baby is clearing the food themselves. It's when they're silent that you need to worry. The downside of being aware of this is your child won't be able to have a nice, quiet, civilized meal without their dad staring at them with a look of terror in his eyes.

You'll also need a high chair. There's only one thing to consider when buying one of these: what it will be like to clean. We made the mistake of considering other things when we bought our first, like how nicely the colours would go with our front room, how comfy it is and how easily it stacks away. Well, firstly, I'm sorry to tell you that colour clashes stop being a concern in a few months when your house is overrun by primary-coloured baby stuff. I know you'll want to avoid it, but you just can't mate, so best to start getting your head around this now. Secondly, a baby does not give a shit if a chair has a cushion as long as food arrives when they sit on it. And fold away? Ha! When were you planning on folding it away? You'll use it at least three times a day – probably way more – and folding mechanisms are just extra tricky areas to clean. Every nook is another half an hour off your day; every cranny is another twinge in your back. You're going to be cleaning this thing more than you've ever cleaned anything in your life. So crevices, fabrics and the like are all just extra things that will lower the quality of life for Future You. Go simple. Stand in the shop and imagine cleaning spaghetti Bolognese off it. Then imagine doing it again. Then a thousand more times. If you have not had a nervous breakdown, this may be the high chair for you.

Right, now you're prepared, it's time to get feeding. Like many of these things, it seems at first like your child might never get it right. Like the whole thing is just going to be too difficult and too dangerous and you should abandon it because there's a whole world of wonderful soups out there that will be more than adequate for the rest of their life. But almost everyone in the history of time has gone through this process and managed it. You don't want your child to be the *one* strange soup dude.

It will be frustrating to watch, because most of the food misses their mouth (and their head) and it feels like it lasts forever. If you are feeding them with a spoon, you'll find yourself putting the same bit of food into their mouth several times before it's gone. They will spit it out, you will scrape it off their face, you'll put it back into their mouth, they will spit it out, you will scrape it off their face, you'll put it back into their mouth, they will spit it out, and so this goes on until you feel like you don't know who you are anymore. But you have to bear in mind that this is the worst it will ever be and, each time you do it, it will get better, quicker and less messy.

When babies first start to eat, it's disgusting. They like to squish it around, press it into their face and rub food into their hands, legs, eyes and hair. Even after they eventually get to grips with where it's meant to go, they will combine flavours that you know won't go together (lasagnyoghurt or Belgian strogganoffles anyone?) and seeing someone do this with food will make you feel uncomfortable. It's gross. But they need to do it. They are exploring textures and what food is. Other animals in nature have much more disgusting eating habits. For example, ducks sometimes get bored and eat each other. So, just be thankful your kid isn't a duck.

Kids' food

I won't try to give you an in-depth guide on how to wean your child and at what stage to introduce different foods because there are lots of different techniques (the general schools of thought being baby-led versus purée-based weaning) and people fill entire books with the details of them. But I recommend reading Annabel Karmel's books on the subject, which are popular and well-respected. They give a really comprehensive and simple guide to what you should do and when. Joe Wicks' *Wean in 15* is another fantastic resource if you can find it in yourself to forgive him for making you exercise during the Covid-19 lockdown. But even a quick Google throws up tonnes of great detailed guides about when you should do each bit, as well the amounts that are right for each age and the quantities of milk they will still need while they are transitioning to the hard stuff.

Just ensure that you wait a few days after introducing a new food to your baby before giving it to them again to make sure they haven't got an allergy or intolerance. You should also avoid salt and sugar as it's very bad for them. Don't give them any honey until they are over one year old or whole nuts or peanuts until they are over five years old. You should probably steer clear of honey-roasted nuts altogether.

DAD TRICK If you're feeding your baby cooked vegetables, it feels very silly to put a pan of water on for two sticks of carrot, so it's a good idea to batch cook a load of stuff and freeze it. Cook lots of vegetables, mash them up and freeze them in an ice cube tray, which makes the perfect portion size for the early stages of weaning. It means your baby has loads of really nutritious, easy-to-prepare portions of food ready to go, but it also means your gin and tonics will be warm (or will taste of parsnips).

It's good to try to get into the habit of getting your child to eat a similar meal to you for as many meals as you can and for as long as you can until it becomes unsustainable, which eventually it will because they will develop their own tastes and mealtimes which are unlikely to completely match yours. (Kids like to eat their evening meal at about 4pm.)

Not only does everyone eating together mean you only have to prepare one meal, but it has the added benefit of making you think more about what you're putting in your body in the same way you think about what your child is putting in theirs. (A varied and balanced diet is essential for a child's healthy growth and development.) This should make you more likely to make healthy choices (but in practice it often means you'll all end up having fish fingers and potato croquettes).

You need to prepare yourself that your child will be constantly hungry, apart from at mealtimes. So it's a good idea to have a lot of snacks in and an even better idea to have healthy snacks, but trick them into thinking they aren't ('OK, you're allowed ONE slice of avocado as a treat.') You also need to prepare yourself for them to show no respect for the food you have spent hours making. They'll probably love the bread you spent three seconds putting in the toaster, but leave the nutritious stew you've been working on all day. This is unavoidable, but it's a lot less annoying if you are all eating the same meal (because you can just eat theirs if it hasn't been squished too much).

Oh, and they will throw stuff on the floor. Lots of stuff. So make sure you've got hard floors or put down a plastic sheet for goodness sake.

Your food

Well, like your time and your personal space, it's no longer yours, pal. The drawback of making sure your child has a varied diet means they get a taste for everything and nothing is safe. Every time you eat, your kid will slowly descend on you like a scene from *Dawn of the Dead*.

The only way to enjoy your own food is to do it without them knowing. So you'll find yourself wolfing down a sandwich while they are distracted (then suffering heartburn for the rest of the day) or eating a piece of fruit hunched over the kitchen bin.

Another option is to use a technique Mark used in an episode of *Peep Show* when he wanted Jeremy to stop stealing his food – he only bought things he knew Jeremy didn't like (linseed bread, Ryvita, radishes) and said, 'If you're going to steal my food Jeremy, I'd prefer you not to enjoy it. And not enjoying it myself is a small price to pay.' There's no dignity or joy to a move like this, but it means you can eat in peace.

Zen and the art of wiping faces

When you pictured what parenting would be like, I bet you thought about the big moments – teaching them to ride a bike, watching them score their first goal, sharing inspiring stories about your life, which they will find really interesting even though no one else ever does – but in reality, these things make up about 0.0003 per cent of parenting for the first few years. The bulk of your work in that time will be cleaning your baby. And it won't be much fun because they will react as if the flannel you're using is made of bees.

If I'm being really honest, I kind of hoped I'd be able to just avoid the cleaning. I don't know how exactly – maybe make sure I'm out of the room, making a cup of tea or something. But, when you do the maths, you'll realize that avoidance is a statistical impossibility. Your kid will have three meals a day and, if they are anything like mine, between ten and five hundred snacks on top of that. Of all the food they have, about one-third of it is consumed, with the remainder being smushed, thrown or stored somewhere for later. That adds up to anywhere between a thousand and a million messy eating occasions a year. If you made and drank that much tea, you'd die.

So, you need to find a way to make your peace with it. It's here we can learn a lot from the Buddhist monks who spend all day sweeping. The boring, monotonous, never-ending task allows them to completely forget themselves, remove all attachments and worldly desires, and enter a pure meditative state. It is only when they achieve this that they find true enlightenment.

Try to see your flannel as the sweeping brush and your baby's face as the monastery floor (and just ignore that the floor is screaming at you). Eventually, you'll forget about the self and become the task. You are the flannel. You are the face. You are the grain of rice up the nose. It is only when you connect with the process in this way that you can be truly happy as a parent.

What to use

We used to use baby wipes and, even though we got through a load of them, I didn't realize it was an issue. Then I saw a thing on *This Morning* about the 'fatbergs' made from baby wipes that are forming under our cities and I worried they'd be able to track it back to our house. They're also usually non-biodegradable, so, even if they don't form part of an evil fatberg, they will probably end up in landfill somewhere, which isn't good. So we moved on to flannels. Both get food off kids just as well as each other.

DON'T COUNT YOUR CHICKENS

It's so easy to fall into a false sense of security. There's nothing more smug than a parent of a perfect kid and, for a few months, I was the smuggest in town. He slept well, behaved well, ate all his vegetables...

Well, reader, if you are thinking 'I hope this prick got his comeuppance', you'll be happy to know that I absolutely did.

What I didn't realize is that babies and toddlers are capable of completely changing their personalities. Instantly. One night, I kissed him goodnight, he looked at me, gave me a beautiful smile and instantly dropped off. I walked downstairs and I probably said to my wife something unforgiveable like, 'People say parenting is difficult, but if you do it right, it's really very simple.'

Then I was awoken by his cries at 5am the next morning. I went in and his eyes, which only a few hours ago looked pale and blue, had turned to flames. He looked directly at me, his neck twisting way more than is natural and let out a scream that convinced me the devil had taken hold. I realized just how wrong I'd got it. Any kid can change in an instant, and it often has nothing to do with what the parents have been doing.

Our child had become an agent of chaos. He just wanted to watch the world burn. Children have these spells and it's often to do with leaps in their development (see below). You can get apps that will tell you (surprisingly accurately) when to expect these and it's all completely normal (and traumatic). One day your kid's personality will change again, for the better.* As if by magic, one day, my son snapped back to his old self.

---

* If your kid doesn't go back to normal after a couple of months, contact a local priest.

YOUR BABY'S DEVELOPMENT

Like men do with a lot of things in life, you might look at parenting as a sport and hitting milestones as like scoring goals. But beware, the moment you score one of these goals, your life will become harder. Every dad I know has been in such a hurry to get their baby crawling, then walking, as if the quicker they do this, the better chance they will have of an Olympic gold medal. But when it happens, you realize that all you are doing is unlocking a whole new range of hazards. When they can only lie on their back, your house remains completely unaffected. When they start crawling, you have to baby-proof all of the stuff at ground level. As soon as they can walk, everything below two feet is now in play to be smashed, swallowed or pulled over, and you start to look at all of your possessions in a new light. That loose change on the side is now a handful of choking hazards. Fancy candles become potential flamethrowers. And that thing you keep by the fire with all of the tools in it is a deadly arsenal of weaponry.

Babies seem to have a desire to injure, scald and electric shock themselves, so you have to make it impossible for them to do so by baby-proofing everything in the house. This means cupboard locks (make sure they never have access to batteries – they are unbelievably dangerous if swallowed), rubber protectors on sharp corners, plastic plug protectors and – the thing that will become the bane of your life every time you want to nip into the kitchen – stair gates. Not only do stair gates have very complicated mechanisms to make it difficult for toddlers or anyone who isn't in Mensa to open them, it seems that no two are the same. Presumably so that, if a toddler manages to learn how to open their one, they won't go setting other toddlers free across the city.

Talking is another milestone that you will be willing to come as quickly as possible, then curse soon after it arrives. It's cute when they ask what one vegetable is. But when they ask what 30 vegetables are in a row and they are all the same vegetable, it will make you want to beat yourself over the head with a butternut squash.

Humping and thrusting

You probably hoped this was an issue you wouldn't need to worry about until puberty. So it'll be quite a shock if you walk in on your baby humping something or (because they have no concept of why this might make Dad feel awkward) when they just decide to do it right there on the rug in front of you.

Well, the first thing you need to know about your baby's humping is it means they are a sexual deviant. Not really. They are just experimenting with how things feel in a totally innocent way. To them, it's just like putting something soft between their toes or a soft thing on their cheek. Uninhibited by the pressure of societal norms, they are just doing what feels good. So loosen up, you square.

If it is a bit too much for you to handle, you can always redirect them: 'Hey, instead of just humping that bear all day, why not focus on its personality?' But really, don't worry about it. The phase will pass and it's not a sexual thing. Unless they quickly slammed a laptop down when you walked in.

Learning disabilities

Some learning disabilities are diagnosed at birth, but many only become clear as a child develops. So, inevitably, you'll be waiting and watching and worrying. Every time they refuse to make eye contact or prefer to play on their own, your mind will work overtime.

As a bloke, it can be your inclination to bury your head in the sand. If any of your child's standard checks come back to show they are behind in their development, you might feel like you are failing your child or simply deny there's anything wrong in the hope it will go away. Or maybe you will ignore it because you're of the traditional 'They try to diagnose everyone with something these days' mentality.

None of these reactions will help your child. If there isn't a problem, you'll be glad to have it investigated and find that out. If there is an issue, it's better to know about it as soon as possible, so you can work on helping your child as soon as possible.

As someone who has been through it, I know it is upsetting. Personally, I thought at the time the best thing to do for my family was to remain positive about everything and sometimes even play it down. Looking back, I was actually in denial. I knew something was up, but refused to make a big deal of it, taking the 'Well, a lot of people are dealing with a lot worse' approach. It wasn't until medical professionals told us that they suspected there were learning disabilities and asked, 'How are you two doing? Because it must be hard,' that I even allowed myself to admit to myself that, yes, it was quite hard.

After that, I carried a tight feeling in my chest that built for two days. Then, when I was driving along the motorway on my own, I just burst into tears. It felt like a weight had been lifted and I could think more clearly about how to support my wife and kids. You will have these moments where it gets too much, and that's OK. You don't always have to cope.

If it turns out that your kid has additional needs, it's so easy to let yourself get overwhelmed by the enormity of it all. You can't help but think about everything all at once, projecting their life forward with all of the difficulties it might cause them. But this will only lead you to worry, which your child will be able to sense, and it will make everything tougher. Yes, a learning disability will complicate their life, but there are loads of other things that will complicate a kid's life that we don't worry about anywhere near as much – the way they look, the pitch of their voice, their laugh, their economic situation, their personality, their sense of humour, a single decision, their intellect – and there are loads of people who have everything going for them, but still turn out to be absolute tossers. So, try not to see a learning disability as *the* thing that decides the entire course of their life, because it isn't. The advantage your love gives far outweighs any other disadvantage they could be faced with.

If you have a kid with disabilities, it's much healthier and more manageable to focus on the here and now. If you can help your child *today* to feel happy, understood and cared for, then you're doing brilliantly, mate. You can worry about next year, next year.

Never underestimate the amazing capacity kids have to deal with shit either. My brother has Asperger's and grew up at a time when no one really knew much about it. There were points when he was younger when my mum thought that this meant he'd have to be dependent on her his entire life, he'd never get a job and he'd never leave home. But she didn't wrap him up in cotton wool and always tried to get him to do the things other kids were doing while supporting him when he needed it. She sent him to a normal (and rough) school and encouraged him to move away to university to study the things he loved. Now he's very successful, happy and he's just moved to Canada to live a dream life with his wonderful girlfriend.

There has never been a better time in the entire history of everything to be born with a disability. We know more than we ever have, we can help more than we ever have and, for all the many, many faults of our modern world, it is more accepting, understanding and supportive of all types of complex needs than it has ever been.

DECLAN (my brother): Every child is different. When I was growing up, I encountered plenty of difficulties: from social anxiety, to never knowing whether what I was doing was considered normal, to being conscious that I sounded strange when I talked. It just meant I had hurdles that other kids didn't. But I overcame them – not because my parents forced me to persevere on my own, but because they helped me to help myself. I now have a job I love and I'm living a totally independent life.

You just need to find out what your child's diagnosis is, what support they need and then give it! I think many parents end up confused and frustrated when their kid doesn't behave the way they expected or hoped. But the key is, especially with non-neurotypical kids, that you can't really know what to expect and that's fine. When you accept that, it makes it easier to adjust and adapt as you go to help your child whenever you need to.

Support

If it is suspected that your child has a learning disability, I'm afraid this does come with the new challenge of getting all of that help as soon as you need it. As great as the NHS specialists are, there aren't enough of them and they are not funded well enough, so you'll be waiting longer than you should be and you will probably find yourself chasing people all the time. Thankfully, most learning disabilities have charities set up to help you and make up for the shortcomings in government help. They can provide assistance while you wait to be seen by the NHS. They know all about the process and can recommend techniques to put into practice right away.

You can also join networks of other parents in a similar situation on Facebook and Instagram. And you always have your health visitors to draw on for support for your child and you, as a family. They can be great for helping to chase things up for you too.

TRADITIONS

In our house, we celebrate Christmas. But whatever religious or cultural ceremony you celebrate, there comes a point when you need to decide whose traditions you will carry forward for your kids: your normal ones or your partner's batshit mental ones.

Prepare for an argument you'll eventually lose where you both call into question the bizarre upbringing the other one has had. Traditions are something everyone thinks they do correctly, and anyone who suggests doing it differently is a monster who is trying to personally insult their values and piss on their memories.

A way of solving this is to come up with new ones together. It'll feel weird at first, but within a couple of years you will have created something special, and filling your socks with Quality Street/sharing a festive watermelon on the roof/chasing a jar of jam down the road will feel like the most normal and special tradition in the world.

Presents

I suspect you will read the following advice, totally agree with the logic and then completely ignore it. But here goes anyway. For the first couple of years, you DO NOT need to buy your baby loads of presents on big occasions.

As I say, for us, the big one is Christmas and we've all been conditioned to think that for our kids to have a happy Christmas, they need loads of gifts. You feel the pressure from everywhere – billboards, TV, Instagram – but a baby doesn't need this. Babies have no idea what Christmas is, in the same way they don't know what Diwali, Eid, Hanukkah or Tuesday are. They won't be upset if they don't get the thing they've been wishing for because they haven't been wishing for anything. They don't know what wishing is. They don't really know what things are. If anything, they will be finding this time of year very confusing.

Look at it from their point of view. For some reason it's getting darker and colder every day and their parents are becoming more and more stressed about something. Then, in quite a worrying display, you guys have brought a tree from the outside and put it in the middle of your front room. What the fuck?

When the day finally comes, you'll expect them to behave in a way that they almost definitely won't because they are just confused. You're telling them to rip off all the wrapping paper in a wild frenzy, when last week you lost your head because they ripped a single page out of a book. What is going on here?

All they want on these special occasions is all they want for the rest of the year (and, by coincidence, all Mariah Carey wants): you. So, please don't feel the pressure to spend a load of money you might not have. Just relax and concentrate on being happy, loving parents. The day when they really will expect a tonne of presents will come sooner than you think.

But what is probably the most convincing argument for not getting babies loads of gifts is how long they take to open them. Honestly, it is the most painful thing you will ever witness. After a couple of hours of this boring charade, you end up just unwrapping all of those things it took you* hours to wrap the day before.

Birthday parties

Let's start by saying that it's highly unlikely any sane baby would actually want a birthday party. Babies generally like sleep

---

* probably not you

and milk. A party is neither sleep nor milk. They are going to get passed around by a load of people they don't know, some of them elderly and wearing way too much perfume, each expecting them to perform on demand and getting offended when they cry. ('Oh, babies never like me!') The baby will be dressed in something uncomfortable and humiliating and they will have to watch the pain on their parents' faces as Mum stresses about getting everyone a drink and Dad tries to politely escape a conversation with Uncle Alan about his dislike of areas that are 'too urban'.

Obviously, they won't actually remember the party either, but I get that you might want to do it so you've got some nice photos and videos to show them when they are older. The thing is, photo editing software will be so good in the future, you'll be able to make a deepfake of the greatest first birthday party ever. Sure, a photo with Great Auntie Joan is nice, but wouldn't your kid prefer a video of themselves doing karaoke with Beyoncé and Buzz Lightyear while Joan is getting off with Alan Titchmarsh in the background?

Maybe you know the baby doesn't care and you're doing it for the guests. On behalf of all guests, please don't. Have you ever been to a baby's birthday party? There's too much cake, not enough booze, they are bang in the middle of the day and full of screaming children spilling sticky drinks everywhere. Also, it's the strangest mix of people you'd ever find under one roof, so the potential for getting trapped in an awkward, boring chat is higher than any other situation in your life.

The only guests that really love it are the grandparents. Maybe you're doing it for them and this is very thoughtful of you, but you didn't have kids to become a party planner for pensioners. If it makes you feel any better, do something else nice for the grandparents or great grandparents. Buy them all jigsaws and lavender bath shit. They absolutely love that. Then you can avoid the party guilt-free and just do something your baby will actually really enjoy – an afternoon of sleep and milk.

Other people's birthdays

Not only do you have your kid's birthday to think about and buy things for, but you are suddenly responsible for all of your child's gifts and cards to other people. Especially your partner. So, from now on, every birthday and Mother's Day until your kid takes a bit of responsibility for themselves, it's down to you to buy presents and cards from them, then write something as if from your baby. Obviously, your partner knows it's from you and you might think that renders the whole thing pointless and you should all just not bother. Well, sorry, it doesn't work like that. I don't know why, but it doesn't.

BOREDOM (YOU)

It's something you might not have thought too much about beforehand, but there are huge periods of intense boredom as a dad. There are the tedious, simple tasks you now have to do every day like tidying up, making food and cleaning everything. But also, a lot of the nice bits of play you do with your kid can get old, quick – like helping your baby put blocks through a hole, hundreds of times in a row. Activities like this do wonders for your child because they learn by doing something, analyzing the outcome, then repeating it. But with your mental capacity, it's probably not very challenging at all. In fact, you probably mastered the star-shape-goes-into-the-star-hole trick within the first 50 goes.

It's the same with books. After a hundred or so reads, *The Very Hungry Caterpillar* becomes a different kind of story; a victim of his own greed, he is doomed to make the same mistakes again and again, and you are forced to watch. It's like an episode of *Black Mirror*.

But if you shift your focus, you can enjoy these things a lot more. Concentrate on your kid instead of the book or game. Even though the task is staying exactly the same, your child is developing all of the time, making new connections in their brain, finding fresh forms of entertainment, learning, improving, getting more creative and, like you, eventually coming to the conclusion that the caterpillar is a deeply flawed and gluttonous individual.

BOREDOM (CHILD)

It's easy to fall into the trap of buying new toy after new toy to keep your child entertained. But if you're not careful, you will end up with a room jam-packed with toys and your kid will still complain of boredom. Then you'll find yourself sounding like a dad from a badly written TV show, wandering around saying, 'You've got all these toys and you don't even play with them.' So, the key is to use the same technique Pep Guardiola uses to deal with the gruelling schedule of playing in the Champions League and every domestic competition: squad rotation.

Here's how it works: separate all the toys into four sets, or 'teams'. On one team you might have vehicles and wooden food (as well as any books or puzzles on those themes). On another, you might have cooking equipment and rodents (I don't know what your kid is into). Once you've got your four teams, store three of them out of the way. These are the reserves and they are going back to the training ground for a while. But don't feel bad, they will get a game soon enough. Now, lay out the current first team in the area where your kid plays. The streamlined set of toys will help your kid focus on them properly and you'll probably notice they enjoy them more.

Every two or three weeks, it's time to rotate the squad, so remove all of the current first team and replace them with one of the reserve teams. Every time you replace the old set with a new one, that goldfish-like kid of yours will act as if they are brand-new toys and they seem to play with them with much more interest and concentration. It's amazing. You can do this more or less frequently depending on how gullible/easily bored your kid is. And you can, of course, have more or fewer squads depending on the amount of toys and storage space you have.

This technique will mean you won't have to buy as many toys as you otherwise would because your kid will constantly feel like they're getting new things to play with. But you obviously still will buy toys sometimes, so here's a tip for when you do: if you're going to get a toy that makes noise, don't. But if you really want to, just don't. But if you're absolutely dead set on it, make sure that it's a noise you don't mind hearing again and again and again, when you're watching TV, when you're working, when you're relaxing, when you're sleeping, when you're dreaming, when you die. It never stops. And the manufacturers seem to set the default volume on everything to 'very loud' for some unknown bastard reason.

Our child got a penguin called Paulie as a present from a cousin. I thought it was brilliant the first time I heard it. He said, 'I'm Paulie, look at me dance!', then did a little dance. How charming and cute. But it really did lose its shine after the first few thousand times. It started to sound arrogant, then needy and unstable. We've all got our own stuff going on, yet this little tosser wants us to stand around and tell him what a good dancer he is. The batteries eventually ran out, but his decline was slow and undignified. He got to the point where he could no longer dance, but still had just enough energy to slur out his old catchphrase, 'Looook at meeee daaaaaoouunnce,' which was very upsetting for the whole family.

DAD TRICK There comes a moment when you look around your living room and see it has been swallowed by colourful plastic. The floor is plastic. The chairs are plastic. The carpet is plastic. There are no family members. There is no dog. All that exists is plastic. So, you need to get rid of some of it.

A lot of people take their toys to charity shops, which means charity shops are an absolute goldmine for toys. So, if you really need to get a new toy, get it from a charity shop. When you're in there, keep an eye out for my old friend Paulie the Penguin. And if you do see him, tell him to fuck off from me.

Cardboard boxes

It's a cliché, but kids love cardboard boxes and it's likely you'll love them too. You'll probably play with the box with way more enthusiasm than you would a toy. My theory is you begrudge the toys because they represent all of the bad things about the modern world and you get equally annoyed when they play with them (because of the sound) and when they don't (because they are going to waste), but you adore the box because it represents an antidote to this. So, maybe it's not actually the box that your kid loves, it's their dad when he's with the box.

One of my greatest spells as a dad was when my son loved to play a game where I would pretend to be asleep in a box, which is perfect for a man who loves to sleep. I threw myself into it with everything I had. And if we put aside any worries about why a child would want to put his father in a box to be silent and still all the time, I realized I had essentially found the ideal activity. I could appear to be the fun dad to everyone while doing what I craved: lying down in the dark. But it didn't last forever. These things never do. Eventually he wanted to jump on the box, which kind of ruined it for me.

Screen time

You've probably noticed we live in a world filled with screens. You've got one in your pocket, one in the corner of your room, and you're probably half-looking at one as you read this book. Your kid is going to grow up surrounded by screens and all of their temptations, so you need to decide how best to manage all of this.

How much?

The general rule with screen time is: as little as possible. The NHS take a very extreme view and advises that before the age of two years old, a kid should have, on average, zero time every day (that's 0 hours, 0 minutes!), then, after two years, no more than an hour a day.

I would like the doctor who wrote this to spend a day at my house. While it is obviously preferable that a kid spends all their time engaging in mind-expanding educational pursuits and interactive play with you, there are moments when a parent has to make food or go to the toilet.

So, while as little as possible is a good thing to aim for, I don't know any parent who has managed to avoid it completely for the first two years. And even if you resist putting cartoons on for the kids, don't be too hard on yourself if you need the TV on for yourself every now and again for your own sanity.

The first thing our baby got into was *The Chase*. The jingle seemed to completely capture him, no matter what he was doing. I once met Anne 'The Governess' Hegerty and told her this, expecting her to laugh her head off. She just told me that she hears this from parents all the time and that it's no surprise because of the combination of the repeated sounds and colourful graphics. Turns out, it's very hard to impress someone who knows everything.

Even though we don't really know the long-term effects screens have on kids, you get an inkling they are something you should limit when you first see them fall under their spell. It's like when you turn a shark upside down and they enter a catatonic state (apparently, never done it) – you can sit them where you like and do all of the things they don't usually let you do, like cut their nails or cook a meal.

You think – this is so brilliant, it has to be bad for them. So, after this point, you'll have the constant mental battle about how much you use your new power; constantly weighing up just how much of your kid's mind you are willing to risk to give you a bit of peace, let you do other chores or stare at your own little screen and destroy your own mind.

The same goes for iPads. They must be bad, surely, but we don't yet know quite how bad. So, you'll probably avoid them for as long as you can, then start using them and get a brand-new feeling of guilt to stick on the pile with all of the others.

JEN BRISTER: Those parents who smugly declare, 'I would never let my child look at a screen...' are the same kind of people who judge you for missing a recycling day while filling their Audi 4x4 with £200 worth of petrol. BOG THE BOG OFF YOU SMUG TWAT. They're also the same people who have a nanny so have never been stuck inside with two feral five-year-olds and an overflowing sink of unwashed plates with a looming deadline.

I am not going to lie to you, sometimes I get lucky and my twins play really well together and, on those heady days, I try to get as much done as I can. BUT on the days when they do nothing but argue, moan and fight and I have to get shit done, the TV is my very, very good friend.

What to watch?

When you are deciding which TV programme to first put on for your kid it's very risky to just have a flick through and see what takes their fancy. Because it could end up being something you'll watch hundreds and hundreds of times. And it could be shit. Even things that aren't annoying at first will become annoying eventually. And most kids' TV is annoying at first.

If you want my recommendation, it's *Hey Duggee*. It's the only thing my son would watch for years and I can understand why. After you've seen *Duggee*, everything else pales in comparison.

It covers a huge range of subjects – from brushing teeth to disability, puberty to bubbles, existentialism to eggs – but without ever seeming 'heavy'. And it showcases all different types of relationships – adoptive parents, gay couples, single parents – without making a big deal of it, which is exactly how it should be done in all TV.

The characters are well-rounded and three-dimensional (although two-dimensional). They have their flaws, as all of us do, but they do that thing that all well-written TV characters do, from Tony Soprano to Walter White, which is make it easy to identify with them even though, on the surface, you are a million miles away from their lives. We watch Duggee and think, 'I'm not a giant cartoon dog that runs a daycare centre for animal children of different species with inexplicably uniform size, but if I were, I'd be *that* giant cartoon dog that runs a daycare centre for animal children of different species with inexplicably uniform size.'

It contains humour that all the family can enjoy and has plenty of jokes that you'll get, but your kids won't, as well as funny details you don't notice until the second, third or fiftieth viewing. They repeat a comforting amount of phrases and actions without it getting to the mind-numbing repetition you see in other programmes and there are some excellently composed songs throughout.

At seven minutes long, the episodes are the ideal length to let your kid have 'just one more' without it making you really late for stuff and there are plenty of episodes to go at (triple figures) so you're not constantly watching the same ones.

Obviously, it's best not to let your kid be totally raised by a TV show. But if you absolutely have to, I can't think of a better role model than Duggee.

Special mentions also go to *Thomas & Friends* and *Tee and Mo*. These are perfect if you're watching in the early morning and need something comforting. The soft voices and relaxed pace are a bit kinder to your scrambled morning brain and the muted colours are a bit gentler on your vulnerable sleepy eyes. *Tee and Mo* is narrated by the soothing voice of Lauren Laverne, so you can close your eyes and pretend you're listening to an episode of *Desert Island Discs*, albeit a very strange one about two monkeys, and they never mention their Desert Island Discs.

If I had to warn you off any, I'd say *Peppa Pig* (brat), *Bing* (whinger) and *In the Night Garden* (WTF).

Your screen time

Before you have a kid, the amount of time you spend on your phone doesn't really affect anyone else apart from you and maybe the odd pedestrian you walk into. If you choose to damage your mind with hours and hours of social media every day, that's no one else's concern but your own. But when you have a kid, this changes. It's very easy to spend loads of time on your phone as a parent, especially if you're at home all day with the child, because things can get boring. You will want to have contact with friends, family and the wider world, and the baby isn't going to tell you to stop. But kids need a lot of your attention and you are in danger of missing out on more than you realize. A lot of the things that babies and children do are very subtle. They will often look to you for cues, encouragement and reassurance. Being glued to your phone can make you miss these little things. It also messes with their head a bit that they have to compete for your attention with this little light-up screen and they keep losing. It's not a fair competition. All of the apps on your phone are designed by tech geniuses to keep you on them for as long as possible. Your baby, with its basic interface, old-fashioned operating system and one-tone colour palette, has no chance.

When it's just you and the baby, it's very easy to convince yourself that it's all fine. But a good test is to imagine that all of this is being secretly filmed. How would you feel watching it back? If the answer is 'embarrassed', it's probably best to put the phone down for a while.

Joining in

Your kid will want you to play with them, which is lovely, and they will enjoy it even more if you really throw yourself into it. But remember, your job is to guide, encourage and maybe label things as you go to help them develop. Your job is not to take over. This can be hard because the chances are you are considerably better at jigsaws, football and building than they are and you'll feel the urge to intervene if there's an obvious mistake. You must resist the temptation to do it yourself, 'properly'. If your kid is building something you know is going to fall down in a few pieces time because the foundations are all wrong, you just have to let it happen. By you shouting, 'You're not doing it right! It's got no structural integrity!' and repairing it yourself, you're stopping them from learning through failure. If you take the piece of jigsaw they are struggling with and put it in yourself, you rob them of the feeling of pride they will have when they eventually do it. I say eventually, because it can take a while.

Your job is to help them deal with the frustration they feel when it does go wrong so they can dust themselves off and improve. Don't worry – you can make a *really* cool tower in your own time.

DRINKING FOR DADS

Your drinking life is going to change, at least for a while. During the pregnancy, you either need to get comfortable drinking alone, be a hero and offer to give up alcohol in support of the mother of your baby, or pretend to give up and drink in secret. None are ideal.

But when the baby arrives, I'm afraid things won't just go back to normal.

The huge mistake many make is to assume you can just pick up where you left off with the booze. But that's like dragging Ricky Hatton out of retirement and throwing him in the ring with Tyson Fury without any training. I learned this first hand when I went on a stag do and began drinking at the rate I always had. I blacked out soon after midday and spent over half of the trip lying on the bathroom floor of a hostel in Hamburg. I think I'd have felt better if I'd have actually fought Tyson Fury. I learned a lot from that and only made the same mistake six or seven more times.

But there are upsides. Notably, the daytime beer. Because you aren't going out as much at night, you're a lot more likely to have a drink in the afternoon. Daytime drinking always has a heightened effect, but combine it with your new low tolerance and you're going to be feeling pretty merry, half a pint in. Maybe that would have been reason for embarrassment in front of your mates when you were younger, but luckily, you're no longer young and you probably don't see your mates any more. So, embrace the fact that you're now a lightweight. It means you get more bang for your buck. And the tipsy feeling of moderate daytime drinking is a real perk of fatherhood.

Hangovers

Hangovers come in many different forms and you might have thought you've experienced them all by this point. Well, prepare for a fresh hell: The Dad Hangover.

If you'd have asked me whether it'd be better to deal with a hangover by staying at home with a kid or going to work, I'd have always gone for the kid. Having experienced it, I think I'd rather go down the mines.

Having a hangover when you're in charge of the kids is like all of the worst parts of previous hangovers, combined. You have the lack of sleep and you're being forced to watch something bright, loud and annoying; you therefore have nothing to take your mind off the hangover. In fact, you probably think about the hangover to take your mind off *Paw Patrol*.

When you're hungover at work, the thought of returning home is your comfort. The thing that keeps you going is knowing that, when you get back there, everything will be OK. But you're already at home. And it's not OK.

You've got someone bored who needs entertaining, feeding and changing. And the physical effects of this hangover seem so much worse because you've been out of the game. But most of all, it's the shame. You're probably used to bringing shame on yourself when drunk, but now it feels like you've brought shame on your family.

Yep, you feel like a real piece of shit. Your kid wants your attention when all you want to do is curl up in a ball on your own because you chose to have Jägerbombs last night. And, later on, you'll have to explain to your partner that the reason your kid has started saying 'you useless bastard' is because he overheard you talking to your reflection.

But there is a plus side to this. When you have your first night out and have no kids to look after the next day, it is glorious. No matter how bad you feel, you enjoy the hangover. The headache, the nausea, it all becomes a real treat because you're doing it on your own.

ELIS JAMES: After about a year of trying to 'have it all' I stopped drinking almost entirely. I found that even a slight hangover made me very grumpy, and children don't allow you to indulge a hangover with lie-ins or a quick trip to the garage to buy a carton of Ribena, so I decided it wasn't worth it. A predictable upshot is that I can no longer hold my drink and, after three pints of lager, I'm standing on the table with my trousers down, shouting about how the millennium bug was 'a right laugh'.

FACED WITH YOUR OWN MORTALITY

Now you are a father, you will probably start to think about your own life in a different way. You will have heard it uttered many a time in a depressing scene in a soap opera when someone has a baby and they need to take a bit of responsibility: 'You're not the most important thing anymore.' And, yes, that's true. Unless you are Piers Morgan, you now have something you will love more than you love yourself.

But it's not just that – you are also being forced to focus on the ageing process in a way you never have before because in front of you, all day every day, is a little version of yourself, getting older at an alarming rate. While theirs is the beautiful blossoming of youth, you can't help but give some thought to your own ageing and it can feel like you're entering a stage of decline.

Their progress seems to highlight your deterioration. I was convinced I'd developed permanent bags under my eyes within the first few weeks of fatherhood and became obsessed with finding a miracle cream to cure it. It was something I spent lots of time and money on for months until my wife reassured me that the bags had actually been there for years. I think we'd just changed the angle of the mirror in the bathroom or something.

Even though having a child doesn't affect your age or health in any immediate way, it's understandable why you might think it because, mentally, it nudges you up the generations. You are no longer the youngest and the one everyone expects to live longest. And you don't want to be. You have someone whom you pray will live much longer than you but, at the same time, you want to be around for as much of their life as you can be. On this note (and, sorry, I realize this will only add to the feelings we're talking about here), it's good to write a will now you have a child, so they know who will get your money/collection of old *FHM* magazines when you're gone.

Your change of priorities can amplify the feelings you're having, too. For the first few months or even years, you, your goals and your health become less of a priority. So, to add to the 'Fuck, what's happened to me?' moment, you might realize you've achieved nothing since your kid was born, other than put two stone on and go grey. But the kid is the achievement. They are your magnum opus; the lifelong project that will live on well after you're gone. You've actually achieved more than you ever have before. No wonder you look like shit.

Even though it might not feel like it when you're having one of those moments, the science tells us that dads are healthier, happier and live longer. So, it's likely you're not deteriorating in the way you thought. You're probably just thinking about it more.

Exercise

The sudden realization that your body seems to be getting worse can cause some men to try to prove nature wrong by setting ludicrous fitness goals. That's why triathlons are usually full of dads who are trying to run, swim and cycle away from biology. While I don't recommend doing this (because you'll start to talk about it all of the time and everyone will find you boring and avoid you), it is good to exercise.

It does wonders for your head. Yes, that's one of those things everyone says and no one believes, but it really does. It will make you feel better about everything, while fighting off that biscuit-podge you've noticed has started to develop around your hips.

Running is probably the easiest thing to try first and I guarantee you that doing it regularly will help you deal with being a dad. Whenever you are feeling sluggish, your mood is low or your partner is asking you to do something you don't want to do, just run!

But be warned, when you exercise, there might be some guilt and some resentment. I've definitely heard mums complain about their husbands 'going for a run because all he needs to think about is himself, the bastard!' Then, the dad will feel annoyed that he's feeling guilty about doing the thing he feels guilty about not doing. It seems so unfair to put your body through hell running through drizzly streets, in an effort to stop it turning to blubber in the hope that you'll live to see your kid get married, then come back to be treated like you've just been for a foot massage. But the key, as it almost always is, is to talk.

Why not explain why you think it's important for you to do it, but also that you don't want to just abandon her, so perhaps you could work out a system that is good for both of you. Maybe offer to have the kids and do all of the chores for a similar amount of time you do exercise each week while she does something for her. But DO NOT suggest she exercises or the drizzly streets will become your new home.

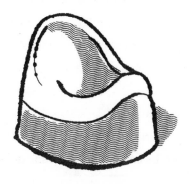

CHAPTER 10
ONE YEAR +

Congratulations, you got through the first year! Unless you're reading ahead, in which case: congratulations, you will probably get through the first year!

You now know your kid incredibly well. They might have started babbling, chuckling, moving around, cuddling up to you and really showing their personality. They are the most important person in your life and you are the most important person in theirs. Or, more likely, the third most important, behind your partner and Mr Tumble. Your carpet is ruined, you have more wrinkles and fewer nice clothes, you struggle to stay up later than half nine and you don't have a clue who is in the charts. But you have someone in your life who you will love more than you ever thought it possible to love anyone or anything. This love is what you need to hang on to when things get tricky…

BIG FEELINGS

Kids' tantrums can be extreme. I've seen my son drop to the floor kicking his feet out, arching his back, pouring with tears and screaming until he could no longer catch his breath, all because he'd finished the cracker he was eating. He had another cracker in his other hand. Your child is really going to explore the limits of their emotions like this at times. A turn of phrase my wife uses when talking to our kids about the wild mood swings and meltdowns they sometimes have is, 'I know, you are having some big feelings,' and I've always found it to be the perfect thing to say. It acknowledges they are really experiencing those emotions and, even if the cause of them might seem ridiculous to us (you dropped a banana, get over it), to them, it's very real. But the secondary effect, and I'm not sure if my wife realizes this, is that it calms me down too. It reminds me that this is just a feeling and it will soon pass.

While your kid is losing their mind because you told them not to eat a stone, you might be having your own big feelings. A child plays with your emotions like nothing else. You will find yourself getting so angry, then immediately feeling guilty that you ever felt such rage towards this little thing you love so much. Undoubtedly, there will be times when your child will push you so far you snap and shout or throw some other kind of strop. This is entirely understandable, but it won't work, because your child won't understand. It will only confuse them or upset them further.

It's natural to get angry when someone is treating you like this. You will have probably never had someone yell at you for hours and hours, non-stop, unless you work in the Virgin Media complaints department. But you can't react in the way you would when an adult treats you like this because a child's motivation isn't to annoy you. They might need something or feel scared or just be exploring sound or cause and effect. ('If I throw spaghetti in Daddy's eye, what happens?')

Don't feel guilty for experiencing the anger, because we all do. It's OK to feel it. But you are always more likely to calm them down by acting calm yourself. If your child is having a freak out and you are there to soothe them until everything is better, their next freak out is likely to be less extreme because they know that it will pass and end in a nice, calm way.

This won't come naturally, but what I sometimes do to help when I am in one of these situations is imagine that we are being filmed for an episode of *Supernanny* and I try to act in a way that wouldn't have thousands of people staring at their screens, shaking their heads. I don't always manage it, but it usually helps me to keep a lid on it.

What's really making you angry?

A tip I took from Philippa Perry's excellent book, *The Book You Wish Your Parents Had Read*, was to ask myself this question if I found myself snapping at my children. We all have particular things that push our buttons for one reason or another, and our kids are experts at instinctively finding those buttons and knowing just how to press them in a way that will cause the biggest reaction. They even manage to locate whole new sets of buttons we never knew we had.

But sometimes we react with feelings and aggression that are attached to something else that our kid just cannot be blamed for. Let's say slamming doors really annoys you. When you hear the slam, you just feel the rage rise. You shout at your kid. They get upset. You feel bad, but you justify it to yourself by saying, 'Slamming doors is annoying' (it is) and 'They need to learn they can't just slam doors all day' (also true).

But take a moment to ask yourself why a door being slammed makes you feel like this. Have you always hated it? Was it something you got in trouble for as a kid? Maybe your dad was a shift worker and a slammed door could result in him waking up angry. Maybe you used to have a fragile front door that would break if shut too hard. Maybe you've always hated how clumsy you are and you're worried this is a sign your kid is the same. Maybe you had a traumatic experience watching the musical, *Stomp!*...or a million other reasons you might hate doors being slammed. Every one of them perfectly valid, but every one of them no fault of your child.

Let's also take a look at the situation from your kid's point of view. For them, this is just another thing to play with and learn about. You actually encourage them to open and close other doors – on books, on toys – so they are trying to figure out why this one makes Daddy's head look like it's going to explode. Is it the size? The material? The volume? Hmm, better keep slamming it to try to figure it out.

Don't get me wrong, it's fine to be annoyed by stuff and ask your kid to stop doing the thing that annoys you. But if you figure out if your instinctive reaction is partly fuelled by the baggage you've got, you won't take it out on your kid without realizing. And it's so much easier to teach them what not to do without steam coming from your ears.

Fatherhood changes you

Fatherhood will bring out the very worst aspects of your character. You'll see yourself get angrier, more frustrated and more moody than you ever have before. But being confronted by these aspects of yourself can be a good thing. It is only when pushed to these extremes that a dad learns what kind of man he really is, what a prick that man is and how he can change to become better.

You'll notice characteristics of yours in your kid too. Or someone else will. For instance, you might say to your partner, 'He's got your cute little nose' and she might reply, 'And he has your manipulative streak.' Seeing these flaws in a little person who looks a bit like you can make you reflect on the parts of your behaviour you need to improve, because you want to be a good role model.

You want kids to do what you say, but they are much more inclined to do what you do. Your behaviour and the way you react in times of stress or difficulty teaches them much more than the things you tell them. If you shout at them to calm down, they won't learn that they should calm down; they will learn that they are supposed to shout.

The best way to teach your kid to be a good person is to be one yourself, or at least pretend to be. The happy accident here is that, even if you're not a good, patient, kind man, you'll end up faking it for so long that you might actually become one.

ROMESH RANGANATHAN: I swear a lot. I grew up around parents who enjoyed swearing and I went on to listen to copious amounts of hip hop, so the idea of swearing doesn't seem offensive to me at all. However, I didn't want to be the parent of the six-year-old calling someone a 'fucking prick' down the park, so I decided I had to not swear around my kids when they were very young. You will notice I am speaking in the past tense as I have since broken that and swear around them quite a lot. I have explained to them that swearing can in fact be amazing, but they need to recognize the appropriate contexts in which to use it. In front of Grandma definitely isn't one, but it has come up.

I have also tried to be less lazy. Before I met my wife, I would happily sit in front of a TV for 48 hours, only stopping to answer the door to the arrival of a pizza. This is partly because my parents, or at least my dad, were pretty good at sitting around and doing fuck all, maybe taking a break in watching the cricket for a nap. My wife's parents were always very active and motivated. She is the same, on occasion annoyingly so, and so I think upbringing plays a huge part in all of that. I want the kids to grow up thinking that being active is the norm, and so I hide my lazy bastard tendencies from them as much as possible. They still think I'm lazy, but they have no idea how bad I could get.

RUSSELL KANE: There are definitely embarrassing moments. My daughter has a habit of getting too hot and just taking all of her clothes off. It doesn't matter if she's outside the front of the house or on a train, she'll get completely naked. She also says mildly racist things, such as, 'Why does that woman have a Chinese face?'

PUBLIC MELTDOWNS

The first time your kid has a meltdown in public, it can be a traumatic experience. Not only do you have the usual distress you experience when your kid is upset, but you are embarrassed and self-conscious. It can feel like other parents are judging your parenting skills, passers-by are annoyed by how loud your kid is being and you're almost certain you saw an old person raise their eyebrows in a way that says 'Parents these days…'

Well, you need to get all this out of your head. To help with this, think about how you feel on the occasions when you see this scene with someone else's kid. I'll bet you don't judge the parents. You just feel reassured to see that other people go through it and incredibly grateful it isn't happening to you this time.

The other parents looking at you don't think you're bad at being a parent because this was them two days ago and they are very aware it could be them again, five minutes from now. They are just feeling blessed it isn't them in this very moment. Your kid's meltdown has just brightened their day!

As for the passers-by, well, people look at loud things. It doesn't mean anything. And the old people – they probably *are* judging you. But that shouldn't concern you; old people judge everything. And their judgement is terrible. Just look at the coats they wear.

ROMESH RANGANATHAN: If you're around other people with children, and they're all behaving brilliantly and yours are kicking off, you know that you are going to be the subject of all their car conversations on the way home. It's embarrassing. Similarly, if you are around people who don't have kids, you know they will cite the experience of seeing yours as a reason why they decided against having them. People without kids, as I did before I had them, all think they know exactly how they would deal with it if they had children, and they think it's incredible that the parents haven't got a handle on it. To them, I say, go fuck yourselves.

Also, the other issue is that the best way to deal with bad behaviour isn't always the most socially acceptable. If your child is throwing a tantrum, the best thing to do is to let that wind itself out. That, however, is not always what everyone wants if they're sitting across from you at a restaurant. If you do something about it, however, you are rewarding the shitty behaviour. When we're out somewhere quiet and our kids kick off, though, I would happily offer them seven PlayStations to get them to stop drawing attention to us.

MANAGING BEHAVIOUR

No dad knows the best way to manage a kid's behaviour at first. All day, every day, you are forced to make snap decisions about what is right and what is wrong. You'll want to be strict with them, but not so strict that they rebel the moment they turn 15, go crazy and start hanging out with the local drug dealers. So, you are constantly trying to strike the right balance and you will second-guess yourself every time you think you might have been too soft or too harsh.

You'll cycle through all of the modern techniques you've read in books that you were sure you were going to stick to. And, when they don't work, you'll fall back on some of the classics you remember from your past or you've overheard other parents using in parks. Inevitably, there will be moments when you use the ones you know aren't right, like shouting really loudly or ridiculous threats you then pray you don't have to follow through on.

I once warned my son, 'If you chuck another carrot on the floor then you're not allowed any more vegetables!' Of course, he chucked another carrot on the floor. Then I had to stick to my stupid word, which he was delighted about. My wife was livid and the kid almost developed scurvy.

One of the techniques we use most is counting. We count to five and, if he hasn't done the thing we were asking him to do by that point, we intervene. For example, if he doesn't come to us to have his nappy changed, we go and get him, often with an exaggerated frown on our face. I know it's hardly much of a punishment, but you've just got to hope they don't like seeing you unhappy enough to try to avoid it. The key with this is to make sure you have a number to stop at and a consistent consequence when you do, otherwise you'll find your child will start running away from you, you'll start counting, you'll still be going into the hundreds and your kid will end up 25 miles away.

A technique we use when things have gone too far is to make them sit down on the sofa and have a bit of time out. This isn't a 'naughty step', but it gives them the time to calm down and reset. We explain why what they did made us sad or cross, then ask them to say sorry and they usually do (in their own way). Although, I suspect they probably don't really mean it. And it probably is the same as the naughty step, isn't it?

These are just the things that we've found work best with our particular children, but they are different spins on the same basic idea: clearly explain what the consequences are for doing (or not doing) something, then follow through on those consistently, giving your kid clear boundaries.

If you have a proper reason for setting those boundaries, it's loads easier to stick to them. And yours will be different to other parents you know, which is fine. If you decide that your kid isn't allowed to splash in puddles unless they are wearing full waterproofs because you can't be bothered washing all of their wet clothes after every walk, that's fine.

ELIS JAMES: We're tremendously lucky in that our daughter is very well behaved, but on the rare occasions it does happen it's incredibly embarrassing. Our son has just turned two and is beginning 'to assert his opinion'. Whenever there is an incident of misbehaviour I find myself thinking 'all other parents on earth would be dealing with this better than me.'

It's easy to forget that children share your DNA, so try to think back to what worked with you as a kid. I was quite sensitive when I was little, which my parents factored in. Loud shouting seems to completely bounce off some kids, but it really upset me when I was very young, and I think my kids are the same. Lots of praise for the stuff they get right, but if you tell them off, you need to sound like you mean it. And, once they are old enough to understand, you need to explain why they're being told off. I think most parents are guilty of getting to the angry stage without prior warning, especially when they're tired.

Praise

What is even more effective for encouraging good behaviour is actually encouraging the good behaviour. It feels much nicer than disciplining your child and hopefully it will make them want to get more of this praise by doing more good things.

You can often turn a negative into a positive with a little shift in the way you phrase something. Wouldn't you find it much more motivating to hear, 'Walk carefully…well done, great walking' rather than, 'Don't run! Stop running!'?

It really helps if you're specific with the praise as well. It's tempting to simply say, 'Good boy!' and 'Good girl!' or 'Well done!' and, while they will like hearing these things, it will help them feel even more noticed and valued if you are more specific about what they've done, for example 'This picture of Mummy is really good, I love how you've given her horns!'

Smacking

Don't smack your kid, mate.

Labels

'Naughty' is a word we try not to use with our kid (and, believe me, the opportunity does present itself), but my wife is a teacher and it's always been a word they have been discouraged from using at work. It's because it's too much of a broad label. Some kids hear it so often, they can get into the mindset from a very early age of thinking that's what they are: a naughty kid. The same goes for other labels. So it's better to describe what they *did* as opposed to what they *are*. My understanding is that, instead of 'You're naughty', you should say something like 'When you throw your toys it worries me because they might hit someone' or 'This morning you acted like an annoying tosser.' See? Much better parenting.

I do make the mistake of sometimes using the word in public and my wife will say, 'George, let's try not to use the N word, people will think we're bad parents' and I'll say, 'Let's try not to call it the N word, people will think we're much worse parents.'

CHANGES TO YOUR CHILD'S BEHAVIOUR

Big changes in your child's life can lead to changes in their behaviour, both good and bad. Let's use the transition to childcare as an example. It's not uncommon for a child to start misbehaving a lot more at home after you put them in nursery. It's possible that this is because they're angry with you for leaving them, but it's more likely that they have spent the day navigating through a new and complex environment, trying to manage their behaviour in unusual situations that are both exciting and testing, so when they get home to you, they feel safe enough to let all of the different emotions they have overflow.

Even though there are these outbursts, the developments in your child's behaviour will generally be good. They are learning about sharing, socializing, joining in and trying new things. You'll start to see these behaviours they have learned at nursery or other childcare and maybe even try to take credit for them. I definitely told my wife it was me who taught my kid to bring his empty plate to us when he'd finished his dinner (I absolutely did not).

You'll see their rate of development increase after you start leaving them in childcare because you've got time away from them and partly because they are learning new things from different people. It's brilliant and it's scary. You'll also start getting reports back that your kid is doing things at nursery that they don't do at home and you'll assume the staff are so incompetent they don't even know which kid is which because there is no way on earth that your child would eat charred asparagus and goat's cheese. He's a waffles and beans man through and through. But it's just a sign that this new situation they have been thrown into with its new routines, people, activities and set of options is developing them and broadening their world. Although, when they are living such an exotic life, it can make you feel a bit like Billy Elliot's dad when they return to your humble traditional home and bland British cooking.

This is the clearest example of a big change, but the same things can happen with stuff like moving house, parents returning to work, relationships breaking down and loads more situations. Life is so confusing and frustrating for your little one. You need to be the thing that makes them feel safe and understood. So, you have to do your best to be accepting, calm and loving by trying to empathize with them even when they are going berserk.

GOOD ENOUGH IS GOOD ENOUGH

When playing Fantasy League, I start every season with huge expectations. I come up with a plan and convince myself that, if I stick to it, I'll easily win the title. It usually goes out of the window after a disastrous couple of weeks, my head goes down and I just give up.

It can be the same with kids. There are lots of parenting techniques that you (or, more likely, your partner) read about before the birth. Maybe you decided you were going to do things the Danish Way or the French Way or the Latvian Way. But then, when the child is here and you inevitably end up straying from the plan, it can feel like you've messed the whole thing up and you think, 'I'll just write this one off and try harder next time, no point wasting all of this effort on a mid-table kid.'

But being a dad isn't the same as being a fantasy football manager. In fact, in some ways, it can actually be *more* of a responsibility. And no matter what happens, you just have to stick in there. Whether you're driving home from another day out when you lost your temper with everyone or you've just been told that they have been biting everyone at nursery, as a dad you can feel really shit about yourself and the job you are doing. But you need to cut yourself a bit of slack. You can't fail or succeed in one moment or one day or one week. It's an accumulation of thousands of decisions, over the course of decades. Today's crisis will be tomorrow's (or maybe next year's) funny story.

When you're in a situation like this, it's good to use a technique I mentioned earlier in the book, which is to try give it all some perspective. I try to imagine my kid as an adult claiming their Nobel Prize and I am asked on stage to say a few words about my genius son. I tell the audience he used to bite everyone at nursery and all of the stuffy academics burst into laughter that this man who cured the world of every illness was just a normal kid once. Admittedly, I sometimes play out a scenario where the same future version of my kid is on trial for a violent crime, I'm in the dock and a lawyer asks, 'Is it true that even at nursery your son would try to eat people?' Who knows what the future holds. Best not to worry about it too much.

Sometimes you'll be great, but some days it's just about getting through. If you really need to put the TV on and feed your kids sweets, then that's what you need to do. Just try to do more of the good stuff and less of the bad stuff tomorrow.

The big moments aren't the big moments

The other important thing to realize is they probably won't remember any of the mistakes you think are huge, but will instead get hung up on the inconsequential things you didn't give a second thought to.

As examples, I have two big early memories of my dad. One is him buying me goalkeeping gloves and the other is him telling me off for not eating a chip that was green at the edge (I'm sure there was more to the story than that), and my stand-out early memories of my stepdad are him singing along to a Van Morrison impersonator in a bar on a caravan park and washing his feet (two separate memories). But both of these men probably did much better things they hoped I'd remember and much worse things they are glad I didn't.

What I'm trying to say is kids remember the weirdest stuff, so there's no use in worrying about every last thing you do. All you can do is try to give them as many nice moments with you every day as possible, to make the bank of nice memories as full as possible to outweigh the others. I still can't believe Dad told me off for not eating that chip.

ELIS JAMES: The car broke down on the way to Margate and I had to change my son's nappy on the side of the motorway as we waited for the AA. We'd jumped over the barrier and he was lying down on a coat that was covering some brambles and it was raining, as cars drove past us at 70mph. I suppose it's not my fault, but I remember thinking, 'This doesn't happen to successful people who've got their lives sorted out.' In that weird way that kids can be quite resilient, my daughter was five at the time and loved every second of the drama.

KERRY GODLIMAN: I know a lot of good dads and thinking about what makes them 'good' is being present. Showing interest in their kids, being open emotionally to them and making them feel loved. That's pretty much it. The only concern I have about modern parenting is people over-worrying about being 'perfect'. Parenting is very much a long game...some days can feel like decades when they're little. You don't get the adrenaline rush of 'smashing it' in one hit like scoring a goal or getting a promotion...It's incremental.

ENTERTAINMENT FOR KIDS

A huge part of parenting is just distracting your kid until bedtime. If they're not eating or sleeping, they're probably going to want to be doing stuff. And that's great – it's how they learn, develop and have fun. At times, it feels like the best part of being a dad and, at times, it feels like the most difficult thing in the world. You can completely run out of ideas and energy, something kids seem to have an endless supply of, as Jen Brister regularly has to deal with:

JEN BRISTER: Most of the time, I get my kids and why they're angry or sad or hyper. That may be because I am tits deeps in arrested development. I love the way their brains work, the breadth of their imagination, their naivety and willingness to believe any bullshit story about fairies, Father Christmas and dinosaur bones that I come up with. But, maybe because I am very much in my mid-forties, their endless energy and willingness and ability to RUN for the sake of running just never ceases to blow my mind. I don't run unless I have to and, when I do, it very much looks like I should stop before something really bad happens. My energy levels are not what they used to be *and I just don't get how they can keep moving all the bloody time.* It blows my tiny mind that they wake up and immediately start talking. I can't remember a morning when I haven't woken to one of them sitting on my chest in the middle of a conversation about dinosaurs or ninjas, '...so Mama, if you are half dinosaur, half ninja that means you could be Triceraninja, which means you would have three horns but also could do great karate moves and...'

JESUS CHRIST my eyes aren't open yet!

They are like Duracell batteries and I love that they have all the energy in the world, but I would also love it if, at the end of the day, there was some sort of switch or plug I could pull out at bedtime so the two-hour 'Go to sleep!', 'Get into bed!', 'Get off your brother!', 'Stop jumping on his head!' routine could be truncated to, 'Lightsoffloveyougoodnight.'

What shall we do today?

When your child develops a mind of their own, this is a question you're going to hear thousands and thousands of times, so you'd better have some answers ready, pal. Your options fall into a few general categories:

Local walks

These are your bread and butter. You'll end up suggesting them every time you can't think of anything else to do. Whatever the most interesting thing within ten minutes of your house is will usually be the focal point of the walk. Great if there's a park, but not everyone has that luxury. At our old place, my fallback plan when I had no ideas was to go and play a game of 'Watch the Trucks'. To play Watch the Trucks, you go and stand by a nearby dual carriageway and stare at it. It served its purpose and my son loved it, but, in hindsight, it was quite bleak and not great on the lungs. So that's why it's good to plan and organize activities further afield from time to time.

DAD TRICK You'll probably cover every inch of your local area on your walks, so it can be fun to pretend to be an undercover cop, keeping an eye on things. And you really get to glimpse into the lives of everyone around you and decide who is a wanker based on fence colour. You can even go to places you wouldn't usually go like culs-de-sac and private land because you've always got the 'Sorry, she just wanted to explore and I didn't even realize we'd strayed on to your land or that the apple tree I took this from belonged to you' excuse.

The planned stuff

A National Trust place, a beach, a river, a hill or a bigger park you have to drive to and you've heard loads about – these are halfway between everyday walks and the big costly days out and they are often the sweet spot. But the key to getting them right is preparation. It's rare that you can pull these off on the spur of the moment. You need to consider sleeping times, eating times and the weather. If well planned, these days can be fantastic.

You will often get the pleasure of witnessing your child see things for the first time. The first time we went to the seaside, my son couldn't believe it. As a real puddle enthusiast, he'd always been keen to splash about in any little bit of water he could find, so when he saw the sea for the first time, it blew his mind. Beforehand, we had worried he might be scared of it and not want to go in, but our problem was the opposite. He didn't want to stop when he got to a safe splashing depth, he wanted to get right in there, as far as he could. And of course he would, because he had no concept of the ocean and how, the further out you go, the deeper it gets. To him, it just felt like his dad had brought him to the biggest puddle on earth, then made him wait at the edge as a cruel, cruel trick.

Activities with others

Doing one of your normal activities in the company of others or just going to visit someone else's house can be really entertaining for your little one. It gives them fresh people to interact and play with and it'll give you some human contact that doesn't throw food at you (like your kids), criticize your washing-up technique (like your partner), yell at you (partner and kid) or piss on you (just kid, I hope).

The trips that you do 'for the memories'

These are the ones you do because you feel that you're a bad parent if you don't spend a considerable chunk of cash every now and again. We're talking theme parks, aquariums and other hell holes that you need to buy tickets for. You will put too much pressure on these and then get annoyed about the planning that has gone into them when your kid doesn't enjoy them as much as you think they should. You'll then spend more money in the gift shop to try to turn this around. This is a problem that gamblers call 'chasing your losses'. Then you'll feel really pissed off when that doesn't work. And you'll go home, log on to TripAdvisor and waste the afternoon leaving a bad review, just because you need to vent your frustration. I can't stop you from having days like this, but I can save you a bit of time with the review, so I've drafted one you can personalize:

> I would never usually leave a review like this, but ＿＿＿ was so ＿＿＿, I had to share my experience. The ticket price of £＿＿ has made us worried we might have to remortgage. Your staff were very rude and I heard a man in a ＿＿＿ costume tell someone to '＿＿＿ off'. The ＿＿＿ were disappointing, the ＿＿＿ were offensive and the overpriced bright blue slush drinks tasted like ＿＿＿. I also think the staff member could have been a lot more understanding when my kid kicked him in the ＿＿＿.

Soft play

The great thing about soft play is that it is all so soft, which means it is incredibly safe for your kid and you can take them from a very early age. It also means that when they are a bit older, you're able to take your eye off them as you enjoy a coffee and panini in the (fairly decent, considering the context) café.

But beware, the relaxed attitude of all the parents is soon picked up on by the kids and you'll notice a lot of the older ones realizing that they are experiencing a limited time of no rules (for reference, see the film *The Purge*). It's not uncommon to witness some shockingly feral behaviour at these places. I once saw a kid shout 'Dinosaur!' then clamp his jaw down on another kid's foot and refuse to let go, as the kid dragged him through a tunnel and into the ball pit. I considered telling his mum, but I was worried he'd go for me next and I've grown really fond of my feet over the years.

That said, if everyone survives, it's a lot of fun and you won't be able to resist getting involved in the rough and tumble of soft play. We remember how fun these places were when we were young and want to recapture some of that rush we just don't get from DIY and watching *The Andrew Marr Show* (as fun as those things are).

But unfortunately, the mild thrill of throwing yourself down a soft slide is soon overtaken by the physical reminders that you aren't as young as you once were. Your joints ache, your bones feel more fragile and, every time you get up from the floor, you make the 'Uuugghhh' sound your grandad always made. It is still quite fun though.

Holidays

Before you have kids, the thought of holidaying with them is a nice one. But after you've been a dad for a while, you become cautious. You've had too many family days out ruined by bad moods, too many long drives made very stressful by meltdowns and your child will have a routine you don't want to risk jeopardizing.

But it's worth just taking a risk every now and again and going for it because holidays have the potential to be amazing. And if they are a nightmare, well, you could've had a nightmare at Tesco. At least with this nightmare, you're getting a bit of a tan and can drink beer on a weekday afternoon.

DAD TRICK Get them into activities that work for you. If you can get your kids to enjoy something you want to do, it will make looking after them easier and mean you get to do that thing you like, more often. Try loads of different activities with your kid you know you enjoy, take them to places you know you like, play all your favourite music and put on all of your favourite TV shows. Who knows, they might really love The Smiths and you've got an excuse to listen to your favourite albums all over again. To my delight, as a baby, my son seemed to love the colour green on the TV. I don't think I've ever got to watch that much football and snooker, then I received credit for it because I looked after the child for almost all of every (Super) Sunday!

GETTING OUT OF THE FRONT DOOR

Apologize to everyone you know in advance, because when you're a dad, you will be late for everything. Before you had a kid, to leave the house you needed to pat your pockets and, in some circumstances, put a coat on. That was it. It could take anywhere between 3 and 28 seconds.

With a kid, you say, 'Shall we go out for a walk?' and, when the time has come to actually go out for that walk, you no longer want to because you're a different man with different dreams, different motivations and you might have developed arthritis.

You'll have to motivate everyone first and, the chances are, someone won't want to go, someone needs feeding first, someone's shoes are wet and someone has shat their pants. It might all be the same person. When you've finally managed to get them clean, fed and in the right frame of mind to come, you have to get them dressed. Socks, hats, gloves, coats, zips, shoes, all with no cooperation whatsoever. Then your partner will say, 'Have you got the bag ready?' Of course you haven't got the bag ready! But if you've suggested the trip, all responsibility is on you. So then you have to quickly pack for any possible eventuality (nappies, food, drinks, wipes, layers, toys). Then you need to get the pram, set it up outside because it's slightly too wide for the bloody doorway (because you bought the stylish but impractical pram – see page 43), while making sure your kid doesn't escape. If you've got a dog, the stress here is doubled. Now the door is open, the remainder of the process has to be completed half in, half out of the house so you've got the added danger of the road to push that blood pressure a little further up the charts. It's at this point that your partner asks you where the blue blanket is. You don't have a fucking clue. You find the grey one. She says that *is* the blue one. You have an argument about how you know what colour a colour is. Then you all need to have a piss. Finally, you load your kid into their pram, get your own shoes on, look in the mirror to check you still look like shit, pat your pockets, get your coat and leave. It can take anywhere between ten minutes and a year.

There will be times when you are tempted to skip a few of these steps just to get out of the house, especially if you are doing some solo parenting. This is fine if you're not going too far, but you can guarantee that the one time you leave the nappies, the baby will shit everywhere; the one time you leave the rain cover, it'll chuck it down; and the one time you don't take the lazy kid, they will burn the place down while you're out.

DAD TRICK Don't tell anyone that you want to go out until you have everything in place. Pack the bags, get the clothes ready, make sure everyone is fed and set up the pram. Then, if it's still daylight and you still want to go, suggest it and enjoy the incredibly smooth process and the look on your partner's face when she realizes she's managed to bag herself the most capable partner in the world.

OTHER CHILDREN

When you get even the slightest inkling that other kids are being cruel to your kid you'll want to go up to them, grab them by the throat and hang them from the nearest lamp post. Then you'll want to take your child home and look after them forever. But this is one of the very difficult parts of being a parent – you have to let your kid experience these uncomfortable and sometimes upsetting situations for themselves. It's how they learn about life. And as difficult as it is to see, the way it affects you as a parent when you know another child has been cruel to your child is much greater than the feeling your child is having.

If you haven't already, you should watch *The Secret Life of…* series. It's like *Big Brother*, but for toddlers and young kids. The relationships between all of the children are very dramatic with wild highs, where they shower one another with love, and difficult lows, where the kids turn on one another and treat each other quite cruelly. I remember thinking how uncomfortable it must have been for the parents of the kids involved to watch, but the explanations from the psychologists really helped. They told us that these situations are exactly what a child needs to learn about people, relationships and the world. Everything they go through as a kid is like a boot camp that sets them up for life.

Playgrounds

I have never punched anyone, but the closest I've come was when I was in a playground with my son. The only things that stopped me were the awareness that I had to be a role model for my child and the fact that the bloke I wanted to punch was seven years old.

It's such an unusual situation to suddenly find yourself in – you are plunged into childhood playground politics, but you're at a disadvantage because you have to adhere to the politeness and social rules of an adult. So, if you see a kid with a stupid haircut push past your toddler to run up the steps to a slide he shouldn't even be on because it's designed for much younger kids, you can't react in the way you want to because you're not a kid anymore. You have to behave like a grown-up, keep your cool, let it go and go home and slag off his haircut in a book you're writing.

But don't worry, it won't be like this straight away. Your first trip to the playground as a parent will be quite a nice one.

Most people start on the swings and you're quite safe here. You politely wait your turn, pop your kid in, swing for a few minutes, hopefully get a giggle or two from them as they experience the fun side of gravity, remove them and you're out. Nice.

But, like all other aspects of your dad life, when your kid becomes mobile and develops a personality, things get more complicated. You'll be at the mercy of what they want to do. This might start with them wanting to stay on the swings for ages, causing you to weigh up whether you should upset your kid by removing them or leave them in there and make everyone else in the park think you are a selfish prick. Then they will start charging around from one piece of equipment to another and you'll be an anxious wreck. It feels like you're chasing around a lemming, intent on walking straight off the edges of high structures and there are a load of other lemmings all over the place, each with their own death wish. Then you start to worry about them too. But you have to let go of that and just be glad they are not your problem.

Some equipment is totally useless – my local park has a square box on the floor that just says 'spin' in it. Some equipment is unbelievably dangerous and seems to have been made with the same attention you gave when creating rollercoasters on *Theme Park World* as a kid, when you left bits of track out and didn't notice until hundreds of thrill seekers went flying through the air and into the hot dog stand. There's an exit to the climbing frame at our park that just leads to nowhere. This is where my kids got to grips with the less fun side of gravity.

The playground also teaches you how fickle kids are. When you need to leave, they will forget you were the person who brought them along to the incredible park and now you're the cruel, heartless bastard who dragged them away from the incredible park.

DAD TRICK If you go to the park when it's too busy, all of the good equipment will be in use and you have to say to your kid, 'Let's play in the spin box.' So, go when it's raining. This doesn't sound like fun, but there's hardly anyone there, the slides are faster and your kid will want to leave after a shorter amount of time because they will be soaking wet. You're winning! (Even though it might not look that way to any passers-by who see you standing there in an empty playground, in the rain.)

How high do you let them climb?

I once heard Matthew McConaughey talking about fatherhood and he said that one of the hardest things is to strike the right balance between protecting them and letting them make their own mistakes. He's right, because your instinct (unless your kid is being particularly annoying) is to protect them from everything you know will cause them any amount of harm. But go too extreme with this and your kid won't have the painful experiences every person needs in order to develop.

We all need to go through situations where there's danger, where we hurt ourselves, where we need to stand up to someone, because that is how we learn how to deal with them. And to mollycoddle and shield your kid from these things is to let them go out into the world unprepared, naïve and vulnerable. You're not always going to be by their side to protect them, so they need to learn to deal with difficulty themselves.

But how high is too high? Well, Matthew said it's clearest when you see your kid climbing a tree. They get to a height where a fall would hurt them and it'll make you nervous. Resist the urge to go to their aid at this point. But when they get so high that a fall would mean a visit to hospital, it's probably a good time to get over to the bottom of that tree.

The idea is to let them make mistakes that might hurt a bit (and teach them vital lessons), but that won't cause lasting damage. For example, let them feel a radiator is too hot, but not a blowtorch; let them have a confrontation with the school bully, not Conor McGregor; let them watch a programme with Richard Hammond in it, but not Jeremy Clarkson.

DITCHING THE DUMMIES

Most kids will eventually grow out of their dummy themselves, but some don't and some take a while, so you might have to get a bit creative if you want to spur them on.

We introduced the idea through the book *Ben Gives Up His Dummy*, which uses the idea of the 'Dummy Fairy'. How they managed to get the concept past the Tooth Fairy's lawyers, I don't know, because the idea is pretty much the same, if *slightly* less weird because she collects dummies and not children's teeth. The way it works is you get your child to gather all of their dummies, then leave them out for the Dummy Fairy, who takes them away then leaves a present in their place. Just to be clear: you do this bit because she's not real.

We did this with both of our kids at once (one was nearly three and one was about twenty months old) because we thought it wouldn't feel fair on the older kid to let his sister keep them, like we were rubbing it in his face a bit. But we also prepared ourselves that this might be the worst decision we'd ever made.

After bracing ourselves for a week of hell, it worked surprisingly well. The eldest had a few tears when we left the dummies out for the fairy, but was quite happy five minutes later when he saw the toy she had left (the Dummy Fairy works quickly) because the book had made him actually want to do it, even though it was difficult. The youngest had no idea what the fairy nonsense was and got a bit upset for a couple of nights, but she was never that into dummies anyway, so soon forgot. And, after that, it was over with and we were a dummy-free household.

But I've got mates who weren't so lucky and I've heard several stories of ceremonial goodbyes, followed by week-long screaming stand-offs where mums and dads have had to come up with even more outlandish reasons to convince them to lose their dummies on the fly until they've completely tied themselves up in knots.

It's worth saying that, as with any lies you tell your kids, the story you tell them about the dummies can trip you or them up later down the line. If they go into nursery and start telling all their mates that they left their dummies at the end of the garden for gnomes to use to plug a leak in their hot air balloon, they are going to look like idiots.

POTTY TRAINING

Before we start this section, please tell me you've not just had a new carpet fitted? If you just said 'no', then read on. If you just said 'yes', then go and take one last look at it, enjoy that colour, that softness, the fresh smell, then say a tearful goodbye, come back and read on.

I'm afraid there is no escaping potty training and it has to be done with every child at some point. You can lay the foundations early on by letting your child watch when you and your partner use the toilet. You have probably already been doing this anyway because kids have absolutely no respect for your privacy. When going to the toilet in front of your kid, you should sit down even when having a piss because this is what you want them to learn to do (and it's a nice little treat).

When you start potty training, you need to get your head around the fact that toddlers won't know when they're weeing at first. It hasn't been something that they've ever had to think about. They just pee as they go, and the absorbency in nappies these days means that they don't even get very wet when it happens. So there will be a period at the start of the process when you wonder how this is possibly ever going to work if they are wandering around and pissing all over the place without knowing about it. But, like kids always do, they will learn quickly.

Success seems to come most easily if you can convince your child to *want* to potty train. You can do this through reading books with them about potty training, watching cartoons that make it seem fun or letting them see kids who they look up to doing it. If they don't want to do it yet, resist trying to persuade them by telling them 'This is what big boys and girls do', because you don't want them to think that getting older is a negative thing that means all of the fun things stop and everything gets harder (even though we know that's exactly what it is).

Because it had worked for us with ditching the dummies, we introduced the idea of potty training through books about the subject, so our child could gradually process what we were trying to do before it happened and hopefully want to do it. This was a bit more complicated in comparison because, if they refused to let go of the dummy, it didn't result in a sofa covered in piss and shit.

We also started to get him to wear underpants instead of nappies, because it helps them get used to what happens when they have a wee or a poo and learn that it feels a bit uncomfortable, so in future they will want to hold it in until they get to the potty. During this period, use 'puppy pads' (the absorbent things you use when training puppies) to put underneath them when they sit down or say farewell to all of your soft furnishings. Pull-up pants are a good transition if you've not got the confidence to go completely nappy-free straight away.

Even though the book technique definitely helped, we still struggled at first and got things wrong. We tried introducing the potty to the house really early – way before starting potty training – because we thought that might help him get used to it. But by the time we needed him to use it, he didn't really know what it was for. He'd been using it as a hat for months, so his parents suddenly telling him to defecate in it wasn't something he would blindly accept. To solve this, we bought a brand-new potty which looked just like a miniature toilet (plastic, by the way, not porcelain – that would be mad) and even made a flushing sound. Because he had witnessed us using the real toilet, he immediately understood what it was for and was way more enthusiastic because he wanted to do the thing he'd seen us do.

It still took a long while for him to have the confidence to actually do it. It can be quite overwhelming for a toddler to use a potty and see what a strange thing their body is doing. But eventually he did it. And, once he got going, he was so proud of himself, he wanted to use it all the time. Then, when it came time to transfer to the big toilet it was pretty straightforward because it just looked like a bigger version of his.

Night training usually happens a little later and takes a while longer, and will involve a lot of sheet washing, but they will get there eventually. Take heart that most of the men I know in their thirties only wet the bed once every few years.

NO ONE WANTS TO HEAR ABOUT YOUR KID, MATE

Something I promised myself I'd never do before I became a dad was to constantly talk about my kids, because it's a subject everyone finds boring. I thought I'd only ever discuss cool, exciting things like bands and…I don't really know what other exciting things I used to talk about. Rollercoasters, maybe?

But the moment you have kids, something switches in your head and you completely forget all of those things you used to think. The child now dominates your entire life and you cannot fathom that anyone wouldn't find them as interesting as you do.

You'll tell yourself, 'Obviously all those other kids are boring, but mine is different. Everyone will definitely want to hear about the cute/funny/impressive thing they did yesterday.' Well, sorry mate, no. They could not give a shit.

Reverse the roles for a moment. Pick a friend with kids. Would you want to hear about how that kid is progressing with their reading? Honestly? Of course you wouldn't. I bet you couldn't even tell me how old their kid is, could you? You might not even know how many kids they've got.

Don't feel bad about that. If we all cared about everyone else's kids as much as our own, it would be exhausting and weird.

No, like your job or that dream you had last night, kids fall into the category of 'things you think everyone will find interesting, but they will actually find as dull as dishwater'.

Unless, of course, the person you are speaking to is a grandparent. They will find it even more interesting than you do. So, save up all of the things you are tempted to tell friends and colleagues, and tell your parents or the in-laws instead. They will love it and your mates' eyes won't automatically glaze over the moment you open your mouth. Everyone is happy.

HERE COMES ANOTHER!

No matter how challenging things might get for you as a dad, there's no denying that children are, on the whole, brilliant. One might be quite enough for you, but the day might also come when you catch your breath for long enough or have so much wine you are drunk enough to say, 'Should we have another?'

Or you might not actually make that decision, but still find out that you are going to have another anyway.

You'll have times when you worry that the second kid will make things twice as hard and you won't be able to cope. But it isn't really like that. The big adjustment was done when the first child arrived. You will go into the second one with so much more confidence and capability. You've spent every hour of your life since you had the first child on an intensive 'How to be a Dad' training course and you couldn't be more match fit. Stuff that you agonized over first time round won't bother you in the slightest this time. Most of the things you'll do automatically and without a second thought, because this is what you do now. This means that, with the second kid, you can enjoy being in the moment a lot more and really appreciate things without so much worry.

Another great thing about the second baby is that the birth is usually easier. There is so much less anxiety when you've been through it before. And most women report everything happening quicker, so maybe don't hang on quite so long at home for the next one.

How soon is too soon?

If you leave it a long time to have another baby, it can seem like it will be more manageable, but you also lose your momentum a bit. When you have them closer, you are in the right frame of mind to tackle it, but, like every old person you pass in the street will tell you, you've got your hands full.

Our two are fourteen months apart. We did want to have kids close together, but maybe not *that* close. When you're expecting a second baby soon after the first, people will see the panic in your eyes and say things to reassure you like, 'At least they will get on' or 'Well, at least you're getting it out the way' (what a bleak outlook on the most incredible experience a human can go through). Other more straightforward folk will tell you, 'Having a second baby feels like you're drowning, then somebody throws you a baby.' None of this is entirely true, but all of it is partially true. It's a lot more intense to have them close together, but it's for a shorter amount of time and you're still in the swing of it from the first.

I've noticed there is a certain age difference, of which we are just on the cusp, where people have a reaction I could've never predicted. I'll tell them there are 14 months between the kids and they go, 'Oh, quite close', then they think a little and say, 'So he was five months when she got pregnant…' and then you can see the cogs turning as they disappear along a thought process which takes them back in time to your bedroom. By the time they've finished, they have a screwed up, pained face and say something along the lines of, 'Ooo, your poor wife.' This happens almost every time, no matter if it's an elderly, distant family member or a person I've just met through work. Every single one of them pictures the complications of sex after a baby.

I know someone who has two kids, ten months apart. I was once at a wedding with them and couldn't believe the amount of people (who, until now, they'd never met) who asked them to describe EXACTLY what the conception was like.

How to make them get along, or at least not kill each other

It's all about communication. It helps to sit down with your first child well ahead of the birth and explain to them that another child is coming along, but it won't stop you loving them. It will just mean that you'll love them half as much. Just kidding. But this is how it will feel to the first one, so you need to be conscious of that and prepare for them to become clingy or angry with you for doing this. Or probably kick off in a million different other ways in order to get your attention. They may even try to eliminate the new child. Scary at the time, but it will make for some hilarious wedding speech material as long as they both survive until marriage.

Try to be as understanding as you can with your first child. This is all so confusing for them. They may accept your news without batting an eyelid or there might be tricky moments where it can feel like they are acting out through jealousy, but the feelings they are experiencing are way more complicated than that. They may be worried that their whole life is going to change, including their relationship with you. When the baby arrives, they will probably miss their old routine and all of the time they had with you, and have to come to terms with their new place in the family. But you shouldn't ever feel guilty about having another one. What it takes from your firstborn in one-to-one interactions with you, it more than makes up for with the extra love and companionship they will get from a sibling. And kids adjust remarkably quickly. If they don't love having a new baby around straight away, they probably will soon enough. It's a new bit of entertainment for them and someone below them in the pecking order of the family they can teach and care for. You will often find they feel incredibly proud because they are now the big boy or girl and they can pass down their wisdom to someone a lot smaller and stupider.

You can't make them like each other, all you can do is encourage kindness, discourage acts of extreme violence and promote a friendly relationship between the two of them. Try to include them both in the same activities and don't play them off against each other (for example, 'Don't do that. Do it like your perfect, talented, attractive brother'). You will really want them to be close until they team up on you. Then you'll do everything you possibly can to break up this coalition of anarchy.

They might hit it off straight away. They might not see eye to eye until they are in their early twenties and they connect over the fact that they had such a weird childhood with you as a father. But siblings will always have a strong bond in one way or another because they are as close as two people can ever be to sharing the same life experience and genetic make-up.

THE FUTURE

Being a dad is hard. When you are away from your child, you will miss them so much it hurts; then, after five minutes of being with them, you'll pray to get a bit of time on your own. There will be times when you think you can't do it, when you think you don't want to do it and, at plenty of points, you'll feel like you've messed it up. But you can't win or lose at being a dad because it's never over. No matter what happens to your child, you will still be their dad and you will still have to do the stuff a dad needs to do to help them.

You will feel like you are winging it at times because we all do. But being a dad – more than anything else you do in your life – is something you are capable of because it's the exact thing you were designed to do. You'll manage it, like every dad has done before you for thousands of years, and your instincts will carry you so much further than you realize. Every day you do it, you learn more and you get better. Just keep talking to your partner, keep talking to your mates, and know that it's very normal to Google 'Is my child a psychopath?' every now and again.

There will be lots of tricky times and annoying moments, and you'll have to do a lot of things which aren't much fun. But as you do it all, something magical happens. All of these things that seem crap – nappy bags, boring jigsaws, cleaning food out of the crevices of your furniture – get mixed in with lots of lovely little moments – cuddles, uncontrollable giggles, feeling your child reach up to hold your hand on a walk, hearing them repeat a phrase they've heard a football pundit say on TV – and the overall result is the biggest, most amazing and fulfilling feeling you'll ever have, and it lasts your entire lifetime. It's a feeling of wholeness that is always there in the background and it's a feeling you can't really comprehend before you become a parent. (That's why, when you try to explain why being a parent is so brilliant to someone who isn't one, it doesn't actually sound very good at all.)

You're undoubtedly worrying about the future. I know I am. It's hard not to think about everything that *could* happen and all of the things your kid might have to deal with, from the stuff that's approaching terrifyingly quickly, like starting school, to the long-term worries you'll have, like if they will find a job they like or a partner they love, then get to have their own kids who will come and mow your lawn for you for free. But it's overwhelming and pointless to waste much time worrying about all of that stuff.

If you are going to think about the future, why not look forward to meeting and spending time with all of the amazing people your child could become? The hilarious six-year-old, the energetic nine-year-old, the conscientious twelve-year-old who makes you so proud. Then, the teenager you can treat to takeaways and embarrass in front of their friends, the young adult you can visit at university and take for a pint (then embarrass in front of their friends again), and eventually you'll get the person who is the age you are now, who is going through all the mad stuff you are going through, and you will be there to give them advice. Then, they will roll their eyes and ignore it because everything you say is so old-fashioned.

But don't spend too much time on all of this. Because the most important, and best, part of being a dad is what is happening right now. And it is all happening so quickly, so try to make sure you don't miss it while you're thinking about something else.

Just enjoy it. It's the best thing you'll ever do.

USEFUL BOOKS

I've read some fantastic books that helped me when I was going to become a dad and didn't have a clue what to do. A lot of the advice I found there has shaped my approach to this book, and to parenting. So, here's a list of the books I've read that I would recommend:

- *Ben Gives Up His Dummy* by Jenny Album
- *Fatherhood: The Truth* by Marcus Berkmann
- *The Other Mother* by Jen Brister
- *Something to Live For* by Laura Canty
- *Dummy* by Matt Coyne
- *Bringing Up Bébé* by Pamela Druckerman
- *Weaning* by Annabel Karmel
- *The Expectant Dad's Survival Guide* by Rob Kemp
- *The Book You Wish Your Parents Had Read* by Philippa Perry
- *Commando Dad* by Neil Sinclair
- *Wean in 15* by Joe Wicks

ACKNOWLEDGEMENTS

First of all, thanks to all of the contributors: Adam Kay, Andy Parsons, Carl Donnelly, Dec, Elis James, Iain Stirling, Ivo Graham, Jen Brister, Josh Widdicombe, Kerry Godliman, Matthew Crosby, Rich Hall, Romesh Ranganathan, Russell Kane, Sindhu Vee and the anonymous midwife. You were all so quick to say yes when I asked for your help and you were so generous with your time and your words. I hope to repay you all one day (through a favour or something, not financially).

To my mate and agent, Andy Leitch, for keeping me in work over the years and for always finding a way to make my ideas happen. And to Ann, Antonia, Amy, Charlotte, Chloe, Damon, Danny, Faye, Flo, Hayley, Holly, Joe, Katy, the other Katy, Kitty, Lily, Rich, Rick and everyone else at Off the Kerb for looking after me.

To Jake Lingwood for immediately sharing my vision for this book and giving me the confidence to go for it. To Julia Kellaway for making it so much better. To Tom Allen for your book writing advice. And to everyone at Monoray for all of the hard work.

To my mates who understand when I can't come out and drink beer as often as I used to.

To David Mitchell, Frankie Boyle, Charlie Brooker, Danny Wallace and Steve Coogan for writing stuff I love to read and making me want to do it myself.

To Laura, for giving me the idea to do this book. And to my parents, my step-parents, my siblings, my grandparents and my in-laws for your constant encouragement. And for all of the times you have helped with the kids and all of the times in the future when you are bound to offer to mind them so we can go to the pub or the Canary Islands for a fortnight.

To my wife, Harriet, for your proofreading, your advice and your delicate way of telling me something is shit in a way that doesn't hurt my fragile ego. For your love, for teaching me half the stuff in this book and for all that you do every single day for me and the kids. While I've been spending all of this time writing about parenting, you've been doing most of the actual parenting.

And to Teddy and Daisy. Without you, this book would've been a very weird creative choice for me to make. So you know, all of the good bits are about you and all of the bad bits are about some other kids you don't know. I love you more than you could possibly understand, and I will do forever.

INDEX

This **monoray** book was crafted and published by
Jake Lingwood, Faye Robson, Julia Kellaway, Jaz Bahra,
David Eldridge, Jeremy Tilston and Serena Savini.